MUSIC PROJECTS WITH
Propellerhead
Reason

GROOVES, BEATS AND
STYLES FROM TRIP HOP
TO TECHNO

Hollin Jones

PC Publishing

PC Publishing
Keeper's House
Merton
Thetford
Norfolk IP25 6QH
UK

Tel +44 (0)1953 889900
Fax +44 (0)1953 889901
email info@pc-publishing.com
website http://www.pc-publishing.com

First published 2006
Reprinted 2007

ISBN 1 870775 147

British Library Cataloguing in Publication Data
A catalogue record for this book is available from the British Library

Cover design by Hilary Norman Design Ltd

Printed and bound in Great Britain by Cromwell Press, Trowbridge, Wilts

Contents

Introduction

Reason has revolutionised the way we think about making music. As computers and technology have become cheaper and more accessible, music software has developed to the point where it's now more powerful and flexible than it's ever been. Reason is the perfect example of this – a virtual rack of instruments and effects, infinitely expandable, amazingly capable. Its global user base continues to grow, as do the number of people producing sound banks and patches and the number of online communities dedicated to helping you get more out of your software.

Part of Reason's strength lies in the range of abilities it covers. For beginners it's a brilliant way to get into producing music on a computer. Self contained and supplied with some great soundbanks, you can be up and running in a few minutes, loading loops and building tracks. For the more advanced user it provides a blank canvas with which to create unique synths and effects, link with Cubase, Pro Tools, Logic, Sonar and others to form a powerful audio and MIDI recording setup, and build complex multi-instruments and live performance patches. Reason is even used in the production of some chart-topping albums, whether it's for laying down initial ideas on a laptop or, in the case of The Prodigy, sequencing most of an album in the studio. Its stability and ease of use continue to win over new users.

Figure 1.1
Reason 3 ships with some great ready-made soundbanks

Info

Propellerhead Reason Tips and Tricks (PC Publishing 2005) by the same author is an excellent way to learn these skills and timesaving tips

Why this book is for you

Mastering the operation of a program is one thing. In fact you won't go very far without getting to know at least some of the ins and outs, the shortcuts and the tricks that are vital to a good workflow. But knowing the nuts and bolts of the program is only half the story. It might make you a great engineer, but won't necessarily help your composition skills. Being able to put music tracks together is an altogether more intangible skill than being able to operate software quickly and efficiently. Music is by its very nature subjective, and while you could easily test how well someone can use a program, it's much harder to tell how good a composer they are. Not least because everyone perceives music differently and has different tastes.

Attempting to tell someone how precisely to make a music track would be almost impossible. Every track in every genre is different, so a music-by-numbers workshop with everyone producing exactly the same track at the end would not really achieve a great deal. But having said that, styles of music do follow broad guidelines such as a typical BPM, instrumentation, arrangements and production techniques. For example, trance music will use drum and synth sounds at a fairly high BPM and be heavily compressed for a 'pumped' sound. Dub music is slower, much more syncopated, often more sparse and makes extensive use of delays. These are generalised examples but show that within a genre there are some broad ground rules that can help you understand how to build tracks in that particular style.

So how does this help you? A question that is often asked is 'How do I make X sound like Y', where X and Y are instruments, loops and artists. So a typical question might be 'How do I make trance basslines in Reason' or 'How can I get a drumbeat in Reason that sounds like Roni Size?' Usually the kinds of music that people want to make with Reason are at least partly electronic, and the styles covered in the book reflect that. Although it comes with orchestral sounds as well as synths, Reason lends itself to more up-to-date styles rather than acoustic, jazz or blues music. The MIDI sequencer approach, drum programming and REX loops fit better with electronic styles.

There is of course no way to answer all these sorts of questions except on a one-by-one basis. But for anyone who is interested in writing music in some or all of the styles covered in the book, it is an invaluable resource which will not only explain how and why to use certain techniques, but specifically how to use Reason to do them. A discussion of programming trip hop drums is fine but if it explains how to do it using the instruments and patches in the program that you are using, it's infinitely more helpful to you. By following the workshops you can see how tracks are built up in Reason, and what kinds of techniques are used in which genres. You can end up with something similar to the tutorial tracks, or hopefully, something substantially different based on how you interpret the instructions.

Most of all you will be encouraged to experiment. Often, the most interesting music happens when you subvert or mix styles. Making 'pure' techno is good, but so is throwing in some drum'n'bass to make it a bit more interesting. And genres are of course not homogenous. Take hip hop for example. One the one hand there's the slick, produced urban grooves of 50 Cent, and on the other the crisp, vinyl-scratched retro instrumental funk of Jurassic

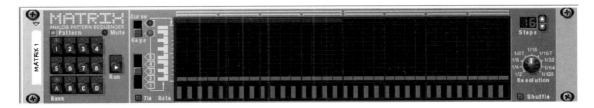

Figure 1.2
The Matrix – just one of Reason's
pattern devices

5. Both technically Hip Hop, but very different. Or Techno, which ranges from the hard acid sounds and huge beats of The Crystal Method to the more original and ambient Detroit Techno of Derrick May, and takes in a huge range of sub-genres and artists in between.

The process of making music in any of these styles with Reason is of course inextricably linked with the technical side of the program. You can't make arpeggiated acid basslines unless you have some grasp of the Matrix pattern sequencer, for example. To this end, the workshops will cover technical tips and tricks as well as guidance on arrangements and production. Whether you follow each workshop to the letter or dip in for help on getting a certain sound or effect, the techniques and ideas on offer will help you to be more creative in your music-making, and learn or perfect writing music in the styles you love to listen to.

About the workshops

How to approach the tutorials

There are eight separate workshops, one for each of the musical styles covered. Each one is self-contained and it's not assumed that you will work through the book from start to finish. In fact you can do some or all of the workshops in whatever order you like. It's not the case that if something has been said in an early tutorial, it will be left out of a later one. If it's a big topic you are referred to the chapter where it has already been mentioned rather than repeating the same information.

Each workshop is designed to give you a good idea of how to use Reason to make music in a particular style. There is of course no absolute set of rules for any genre, although some have characteristics like instrumentation and tempo to call their own. Each workshop looks at a brief history of the genre, some notable artists and recommended listening before taking you through some examples of how to go about writing that type of music in Reason.

Within each one you are encouraged to experiment and try your own things. A genre can contain very wide variations on a basic theme, and you'll get the most out of the workshops by building on the examples and techniques shown, experimenting and making the tracks your own. The emphasis is on linking musical styles with the technical operation of Reason, and how to make the technology work for you, firing your creativity rather than slowing you down. It's not just about the nuts and bolts of the program but also how to think about instrumentation, tempo, themes, structure and production. Where a sound or technique is heavily used by a particular artist they are mentioned, in order to better illustrate the point and make it clearer what kind of sound you may want to aim for.

It's important to understand how the referencing works in the workshops. At various points, you are given a file reference number. What this refers to is the fact that if you open the associated project file at the time you get to it in the text, everything that's been discussed up to that point will have been done in that project file. Here's an example. Let's say you are doing the Techno workshop and you get to step 4. The instruction (like the one in the margin on the left) says 'File stage 3'. This means that everything described in steps 1, 2 and 3 is contained in the Techno Reason file called 'stage 3'. Everything you are about to do in step 4 will be present in file 'stage 4', but you shouldn't open that until you have done step 4, so you can see how it should have turned out. This system applies throughout all the workshops. Of course each set of files is kept in a separate folder, sorted by style. It goes without saying that when working on the trip hop chapter, you should use the project files in the trip hop folder. The dub files are all in the dub folder, and so on.

File stage 3

Very important

When you load the project files you may be told that some of the ReFills are missing. This is misleading. If you have downloaded the ReFills from the website you will need to point Reason at them the first time you open the files. This is because Reason will need to know the relative path to the ReFill on your hard drive. Due to the nature of the way Reason references external files, it's impossible to fix this problem without putting everything in a single folder, which is impractical for our purposes. The good news is that it will only happen the first time you open a file. After that, if you save it, Reason will know where the files are. The files aren't protected, so you can save them locally. Here's what to do:

• If presented with a 'Missing Sounds' dialogue box when you open a file, click the Browse button and navigate to the ReFill that Reason is looking for. It should then remember where it is.

Also, a more permanent solution is this.

• In the Browser, add the ReFills folder containing the tutorial ReFills you have downloaded to your Favourites list on the left of the Browser window. Once Reason knows that the folder full of ReFills is in the favourites list, it shouldn't have any problems finding external files.
• A finished version of each track is also provided as an .rps file that you can experiment with but not save.

Online resources

As well as the Reason sound banks that you will already have, there are a number of ReFills and REX files available for download from the PC Publishing website. The workshops will reference these ReFills, so it's important that you download them if you can. An online resource is better than a CD as it doesn't get lost or scratched, and it also allows us to provide different versions of the project files for each workshop. You will see that for each workshop there are several project files available for download representing different stages of the composition. If you're unsure about how the project should be looking and sounding, you can always jump in halfway through by loading the relevant project file. If you prefer, you can work through the projects step-by-step, opening each successive stage of a project as a new file to see how all the things in the previous step have been implemented. There are enough project files for each workshop so that there are never more than a few new additions in each one, and you won't get lost. An online resource also lets us maintain a useful list of links and other information that can be easily updated. Hopefully your tracks won't sound exactly the same as the finished tutorial files, which will mean you have stamped your identity on them and made them your own.

The URL to go to is http://pc-publishing.com/reasonprojects. You will be required to log in with the username : 'mppr-reader' and the password 'malstrom', both without the quotes.

Some things to remember

Although the tutorials will cover 'pure' forms of musical styles, they will also touch on the many variations that exist within them. If you want to make honest-to-goodness hardcore Drum & Bass that's great. Alternatively you might want to do something lighter with acoustic instruments but still with sped-up beats. A lot of really interesting music comes from people subverting and mixing styles, so you shouldn't feel compelled to stick strictly to straight-down-the-line, undiluted styles. Unless of course you want to. Some of the styles on offer have been influenced by or even spawned by others that we cover, so nothing is mutually exclusive. It's mostly related, even if it means tracing back a generation or two. The key is to take on board the tricks and techniques in the workshops and then expand on them and use them in the production of your own music.

Although you can follow the tutorials step-by-step, opening each stage of a project as a new file, it's hoped that you will add at least some of your own input, if not work entirely from scratch, using the tips in the workshops for guidance rather than as a strict template.

If you are planning to use the workshop files to see precisely how the techniques and tips in the workshops have been done, you'll need to download the three zipped ReFill folders from the website as well as the Reason project

Name	Date Modified	Size	Kind
stage 1.rns	19 October 2005, 15:03	24 KB	Reason Song
stage 2.rns	19 October 2005, 15:43	88 KB	Reason Song
stage 3.rns	19 October 2005, 16:25	188 KB	Reason Song
stage 4.rns	19 October 2005, 16:54	196 KB	Reason Song
stage 5.rns	19 October 2005, 17:40	224 KB	Reason Song
stage 6.rns	19 October 2005, 19:14	244 KB	Reason Song
stage 7.rns	21 October 2005, 16:35	244 KB	Reason Song
stage 8.rns	21 October 2005, 17:00	248 KB	Reason Song
stage 9.rns	21 October 2005, 17:12	316 KB	Reason Song
stage 10.rns	21 October 2005, 17:28	320 KB	Reason Song

Figure 1.3
Step by step project files are provided online for you to download

files. They contain many loops and patches, and will definitely provide you with some great new sounds as well as helping you through the workshops.

When the workshops mention the 'Sound Bank', they are referring to the Reason Factory Sound Bank. You will have installed this when installing Reason, as it will no longer run without your having done so.

Whenever a patch or a file is mentioned (as they frequently are) it is usually pointed out exactly where it can be found. If you are having trouble finding something, you can use the search field in the Browser window to locate it. Remember it will usually search the folder you're currently looking at, so to search a whole ReFill or folder, first navigate to its top level.

The mixes and arrangements of the finished workshop files are in no way meant to be considered absolute. They are merely an example of how a track could turn out. Although they guide you on instrumentation, arrangement and melody, it would be pointless to tell you what notes to play! That wouldn't really get you anywhere. Instead, listening to the examples in the project files and seeing what notes have been used is a much better guideline as to what you might want to try. Remember also that mixing is very subjective and will depend on your own ears and setup. A mix that sounds good on big speakers might sound bad on headphones, and vice versa. This is why it's recommended to test a mix on multiple systems until it's as even as it can be. You are of course in no way limited to the sounds and patches on offer. If you have your own, use those too!

There are usually several ways to achieve the same thing in Reason. For example, to create a device you can use the Create menu from the toolbar or right click / control+click to bring up the contextual menu and choose Create from there. There's no right or wrong method to choose, although you'll almost certainly get used to doing things in the way that suits you.

Although some of the steps will work in Reason 2.5, every workshp is designed to be run in Reason 3. You may not be able to open the files in anything earlier than Reason 3. Plus, some are dependent on the Combinator and various new features and sounds only introduced in v3. Basically, you need Reason 3.

Thanks

The author would like to thank those companies who donated their excellent ReFills and REX files for inclusion in the workshops. If you like the demo versions, please consider purchasing the full versions for a much wider set of loops and patches. In no particular order:

PowerFX – www.powerfx.com
AMG - www.amguk.co.uk
Zero-G - www.zero-g.co.uk

For more information on this see the PC Publishing website at:
http://www.pc-publishing.com/reasonprojects.

Setting up

Before you start

You may already have a computer, or you could be looking to buy one to start making music with. Modern music software is fairly demanding of a computer's resources, so it makes sense to get some capable hardware and set it up correctly. Luckily, Reason's system requirements are considerably lower than those of many other sequencers. This is partly because it is self-contained, and because of that the programmers can fine tune it for maximum performance and stability. But even though the minimum system requirements are relatively low, it's still advisable to get a powerful computer. Remember that minimum requirements are just that – the minimum needed to run properly. For better performance, get the best package you can afford. The great thing about Reason is that it lets you run as many instruments and effects as your hardware can handle, so the better the hardware, the fewer limitations you will have when it comes to creating music.

Here are some factors to consider when choosing a computer for audio work:

- Processor speed.
- Hard drive size
- RAM capacity
- Expansion options
- Fan noise
- Monitor size and type

Whilst most new computers probably meet the minimum system requirements for Reason, there are a number of arguments for buying one with a better specification.

- The faster the CPU, the more effects and instruments you can run.
- A larger hard drive can store more data and helps modern operating systems to run better
- More RAM means better sample playback, and generally benefits the running of a computer
- PCI and drive slots as well as USB and FireWire ports allow more flexibility to use audio and MIDI interfaces and add external hard drives. PCMCIA slots in laptops let you fit high quality sound cards directly into the computer

- A quieter computer is less likely to interfere with live recordings in other software such as Cubase.
- A flat LCD screen is much easier on your eyes during prolonged work sessions, generates far less heat and takes up much less space than a traditional CRT monitor

Mac or PC

This is a long-running debate with strong advocates on either side, but the sensible view is that both have their relative merits. Increasingly for musicians your choice of platform is determined by your preferred sequencer. Logic, for example, is now Mac only. Sonar by contrast is PC only. Reason runs on either platform, and the feature set on both is identical. Version 2.5 even still runs on Mac OS9, which is rare these days as the Mac world has mostly migrated to using OSX. A few studios have stuck with OS9 for various reasons, but OS9 support isn't present in version 3.

A brief comparison of Macs and PCs

High end Macs can to be more expensive to buy initially, although prices have dropped considerably in recent years. The Mac Mini as shown in Figure 2.1 represents a surprisingly cheap and powerful entry-level Mac. Mac OSX tends to be very stable, and is not prone to infections by viruses. When you buy a Mac you know that it has been built to a specification set by Apple, and so hardware / software conflicts are rare. Peripherals often run without any additional drivers, and as an aside, Macs look good too!

Figure 2.1
Apple's Mac Mini is a low-cost but powerful entry-level system for running music applications.

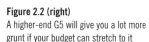

Figure 2.2 (right)
A higher-end G5 will give you a lot more grunt if your budget can stretch to it

Figure 2.3
PCs can be built to order from various components. More choice, but beware driver conflicts.

Windows PCs are generally cheaper to buy, and building or buying one made of components you specify yourself is fairly straightforward. PC shops are found in every town, and Windows 2000 and XP are very widely used. On the flipside, a PC is more at the mercy of the drivers written for its components to allow them to talk to each other. A bad driver can throw a real spanner in the works. Troubleshooting Windows can require a lot of technical knowledge, and it is prone to viruses, unlike the Mac. A number of specialist audio PC companies sell ready-made packages and will also custom-build you a PC or a laptop based on your specifications. This makes it easy to get exactly the deal you're looking for. It's worth using specialists as they usually pre-configure and optimize the PC for audio work.

A lot of people stick with what they know, and ultimately it's personal preference that will dictate your choice of platform. Luckily, Reason works well on both and project files are cross-platform so moving Reason projects between Mac and PC is no hassle.

Tip

Keep your operating system up to date with regular software updates. Reason tends to takes OS updates in its stride, and doesn't often experience problems or glitches with incremental system changes. Reason 3 has been updated more frequently than earlier revisions, so be sure to check the Propellerhead website for the latest version.

Installing Reason

You will probably need to be logged in as an Administrator when installing. However, under Mac OSX, Windows 2000 or Windows XP on your own computer, your regular account will probably be an admin account anyway.

Any recent Mac will be running OSX. Unless you have a specific reason on an older Mac, don't install the OS9 version of Reason 2.5. It will install and probably run, but only in Classic mode. This is not a good way to work. Only use Classic if your chosen application doesn't exist for OSX. Reason 3 doesn't support OS9.

On the Mac

Installation is fairly straightforward. Double clicking the installer icon runs you through the process. When installing Reason 2.5 on the Mac, choose Easy Install to install the Program, Factory and Orkester Sound Banks. Reason needs at least one sound bank present to work. If you don't install the Factory Bank now, it will ask for you to insert the CD every time you run the program. The Sound Banks take up around 530MB each, and have all the sounds you need to get started. If you don't want to install the sound banks, or are returning later to install a sound bank you omitted earlier, choose Custom Install. By checking or unchecking the boxes you can specify which to leave or include. If you just install the program at first, you can drag and drop the Sound Banks to your hard drive later. The other two CDs just contain these ReFills, and drag and drop works as well as using the installer.

If you are installing Reason 3 you will be prompted to insert the sound bank CDs on first install. You do not have the choice to install them later - the installer will not complete without them.

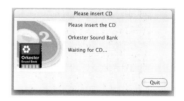

Figure 2.4
Choose where to install Reason and its sound banks on the Mac

Where to go

From the installer you can select which drive to install the files to, if you have more than one hard drive. By clicking Select Folder you can choose a subfolder from a drive.

On Windows

Windows 2000 and XP will probably autorun the Reason installer. If not, go to the start menu and select Run, then type d:/ or whatever the name of your optical drive is. Alternatively, go to My Computer > Program Disc. Then double click the Install Reason icon. It's a good idea to quit all other running programs before starting the installer.

Location, location

With Reason 2.5, Windows asks whether you want to install the Sound Banks, and if so, where. If for any reason you don't want to install them, or want to put them somewhere other than the default location, use the dropdown menus next to their names to specify this. In Reason 3, you have to install the sound banks at the time of installation. In fact there's no option to do this later.

Figure 2.5
Windows gives you the option to install Sound Banks now or later

Figure 2.6
The contents of the Reason folder on a PC

Preferences

Reason's preferences determine how it interacts with your system and what settings it should use. They also let you tweak Reason for specific purposes. The most important are the audio and MIDI settings, as they control how Reason receives and transmits all its data. Here is a look how you could set the preferences.

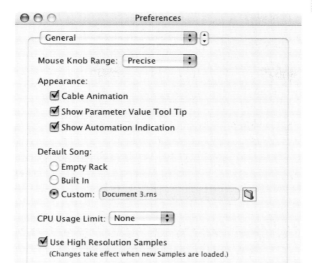

Figure 2.7
Reason's preferences

General

This contains general settings for Reason's operation. The Appearance settings are a matter of personal choice, whether you want cables to animate and tooltips to appear. These are usually best left switched on.

The default song option lets you specify what Reason should do when you boot it up each time. By default it opens an empty rack, a blank canvas for you to start with. Selecting Built In opens the standard Reason demo song - which is a bit pointless to have open every time you start it up. The most useful option here is to select Custom, and use the file browser button to navigate to a project file. Let's say you always or more often than not work with the same kind of setup. A typical example of this might be a mixer, some reverbs and compressors, a piano and some drums and a bass loaded into various instruments. Rather than having to manually add these each time, create a template song with all the modules set up but no MIDI recorded, and save it as a file called something like basictemplate.rns. If you set Reason to open this file on startup you'll save time setting up a new rack every session.

Tip

Remember, if using a template song, to save it as a new file name rather than just pressing save, or you'll save over your template.

Tip

A good way to avoid accidental overwriting of template files is to make the templates read-only, preventing saving. On the Mac, use Get Info for a file and change its Ownership and Permissions to Read Only. On a PC control + click the file, select Properties and change its attributes to Read-Only.

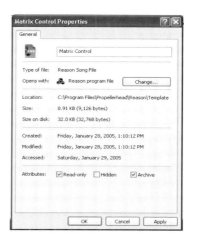

Figure 1.8
Telling Windows that a file is Read-only

The CPU usage limit menu tells Reason at what point it should stop demanding more power from your processor. On a slower machine you may want to impose a limit, especially if you are running other software alongside Reason, so that it doesn't drain the system too much. Limiting it to 80% of the CPU would ensure it left some capacity for the other programs. In reality though, Reason is much kinder to processors than many other sequencers. Even on a moderately powered machine you will be able to switch this setting to No Limit and probably not notice any adverse effects. As all processing is done in-house, (inside Reason) the programmers have been able to optimize it for maximum CPU efficiency. On a modern machine you can leave the High Resolution Samples option switched on as well, as it's unlikely to trouble your computer.

Figure 2.9
Specifying a CPU usage limit – or not

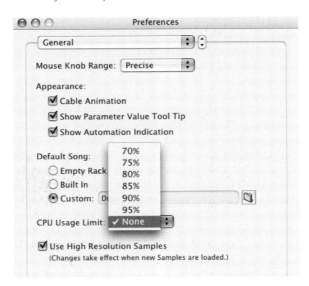

Audio

This is where you tell Reason which device to use to transmit sound. The Master Tune control will alter the main tuning setting for the whole program. In practice you'll almost certainly never need to use this. The great thing about computer sequencers is that you can be sure they're always in tune. The only reason to use it would be in a situation where you had to match a Reason track to other recorded material that had itself been recorded out of tune.

Under the Audio Card setting you choose which device to use to fire sound out of Reason. In practice you'll probably only have one sound card active, and you should choose it from the list.

Tip

If you're just getting started and can't get any sound output, check that the program is set to use your sound card and isn't set to No Sound. Also check that your card drivers are up to date and that the volume is turned up.

Tip

Mac users - if you're having trouble getting sound output, switch the preferences to use Built In Audio. All Macs have an internal soundcard and at least one speaker as standard. If you can get sound out of the Mac speaker but not the third-party soundcard, the problem isn't with Reason but with the settings of the other card. On PC or Mac you can always try plugging headphones into the built-in soundcard to test at which stage in the signal path a fault is occurring.

The Sample Rate option is based on the available rates supported by your soundcard. Standard cards will support up to 44.1kHz, higher spec ones up to 96kHz and some even up to 192kHz. As a rule of thumb, work at 44.1kHz, as this is CD quality. 48kHz is the standard for DAT and DVD but you can encounter issues when moving files to hardware with different capabilities. Usually this involves a track playing slower or quicker than it should for no apparent reason. The way around this is to resample the track to a sample rate supported by the new hardware. Equally, there's no real point in working at a sample rate of less than 44.1kHz unless you have a specific reason to do so.

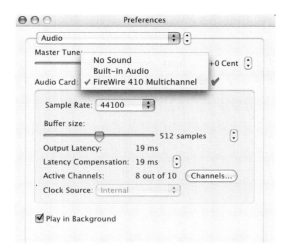

Figure 2.10 (left)
Choosing a soundcard for Reason to use

Figure 2.11 (below)
Setting the sample rate

The buffer settings control the streaming of audio between software and hardware. Buffer size is important because it affects the latency of MIDI and the reliability of audio. Latency is a small but annoying gap between your pressing a key and hearing the sound. Too much latency can make it impossible to play in time. Setting a lower buffer size reduces the latency but also increases the risk of pops and clicks in the audio playback. Raising the buffer size increases latency but makes for improved audio performance. As all hardware setups are different there's no strict rule of thumb for what setting to use, although a buffer size of 256 or 512 samples is often a good bet. Experiment with settings to see what works best and gives you minimum latency but maximum audio quality.

Figure 2.12
Buffer sizes affect latency

Latency tip

Here's a good rule of thumb : when you're playing MIDI in a lot and writing music, use a lower buffer setting to get minimum latency. Then when you're arranging and mixing, increase the buffer size to improve audio performance. If you're not playing notes in any more the latency won't be an issue.

Tip

Latency is a particular problem with lower-end PC laptops. Often the standard soundcard isn't up to the job of running serious audio applications. In this case, an external USB or FireWire, or special laptop PCI audio card is the solution. Mac laptops tend to have better soundcards as standard, but still often benefit from the introduction of something a bit more specialised.

Reason supports up to 64 channels of audio output. You can see them on the Audio Out module at the top of the rack. If your audio interface supports more than two output channels, you can activate them in the audio preferences box

Tip

If you tick the Play in Background option, you'll be able to play sound from Reason even when the program is hidden or behind another program.

Figure 2.13
Sound drivers on Windows

and connect instruments or mixers to them. Sound will then be routed to the hardware outputs on your interface as you decide in the preferences.

A note about audio drivers

On Windows, audio hardware will have an ASIO driver supplied with it. Choose this driver to use with the device. Alternatively, use the DirectX or ASIO multimedia driver, but only if a specific ASIO driver isn't available.

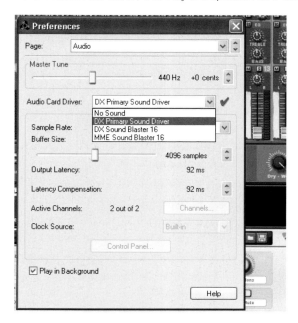

On Mac OS 9, audio hardware will have a dedicated ASIO driver which you should select. On Mac OSX, CoreAudio should be selected to use the internal audio hardware, or the specific driver that controls your third-party device should be selected. For example if you have an M-Audio Audiophile USB, its name will appear as an option in the list for you to choose.

MIDI settings

In Reason 2.5

From the dropdown menu you can select which device to use for MIDI input. In many cases this will be the same as the audio device, as most cards offer both audio and MIDI in and out. If you have separate audio and MIDI devices, Reason will happily use them both at the same time. There are 16 standard MIDI channels but a safe bet is to use channel 1 on all your devices when setting up communication.

Advanced MIDI lets you configure Reason to receive MIDI input from external sources for the purpose of remote control or sync. Usually you will have one MIDI interface handling all communication so that is the one to choose. If you're not syncing Reason or hooking it up to any external sequencers you don't need to worry about these settings.

Tip

A good way to check that MIDI is being received is to hit some notes on the keyboard and look at the channel 1 section of Reason's MIDI panel. You should see a red light blink when you play. If not, check your keyboard is sending on channel 1 and Reason is receiving from the correct device on channel 1.

In Reason 3

Reason 3 does away with the MIDI tab and replaces it with one called Control Surfaces and Keyboards. This is because it has a new system of handling MIDI communication called Remote. Instead of reading from a single device, Reason 3 can now receive data from multiple MIDI controllers at the same time. The point of this is to make it much easier to play your Reason system. Instead of being predominantly a studio tool it can now be used much more easily for live performance as well. Many people have a USB MIDI controller keyboard, or a standard keyboard with realtime controllers like knobs and sliders. Reason 3 has built-in support for a wide range of controllers from leading manufacturers, and allows you to customise setups for keyboards that aren't supported out of the box. Support for new models will be added as they come onto the market. As templates are stored in a folder outside the program itself, this will not require any program updates but rather a simple drag-and-drop. Here are some things to note about the Remote system.

Figure 2.14
Detecting MIDI devices in the MIDI preferences

When you install and boot Reason 3 for the first time it will scan your system for any installed drivers relating to MIDI controller devices. If you are adding devices with drivers later, there is an auto-detect button on the Preferences > Control Surfaces dialogue box.

If Reason does pick up such a device, it will automatically map its realtime knobs and sliders to the most useful controls on whichever module in the rack you select. Typically, sliders will correspond to mixer channels or filter controls on an instrument. Knobs on a keyboard will probably be mapped to filter or pan controls. You can remap these, but for everyday purposes the default settings are useful.

In the list of attached surfaces you can specify by ticking or unticking the box whether each should be used with Reason. You may have a controller accessing another program and not want it to interfere with Reason. In this situation, uncheck the box. The Add, Edit and Delete buttons let you manage your list of controllers.

Figure 2.15
Use the Auto-detect button if your model is not recognised

Figure 2.16
Use multiple control surfaces or keyboards

If your MIDI keyboard is not picked up, or is connected via a MIDI interface rather than USB or FireWire, you can make Reason pick it up by clicking the Add button. Select the manufacturer or choose Other if it isn't displayed. Then from the Model menu choose what kind of keyboard it is. If your MIDI interface is not automatically picked up, press the Find button and press a key on the keyboard. Using MIDI Learn, Reason will pick it up and remember it.

Tip

If you select a controller device from the list of available models, look out for any information that is displayed next to its picture in the Control Surface setup window. Some devices have idiosyncrasies that need to be remembered when setting up, such as a particular setting that has to be made or a channel that has to be active.

Figure 2.17
Locking MIDI devices to modules in the rack

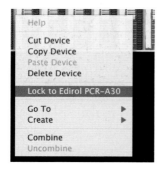

The more realtime controllers you have on your keyboard, the better your control over Reason will be. A small keyboard will offer basic controls, but a bigger one like the M-Audio Keystation Pro 88 or a dedicated control surface like a Mackie Control will give you much more comprehensive options if you happen to own one. Reason 3 even supports motorized faders and device naming on dedicated control surfaces.

The way to manage the multiple devices is to lock them to devices in the rack. The controller specified as the Master Keyboard in the preferences will always follow the MIDI input (i.e. play whichever module you select in the rack). However, any number of subsequent controllers can be added. By selecting Options > Surface Locking you can select any available controller and lock it to any available module. This means it will always just play that module, at least until you unlock them from each other. The Master Keyboard can't be locked, unless you specify that Reason should not use a Master keyboard. This is a bit limiting however as it would mean you couldn't easily flick between playing the different modules.

In Use

By having more than one control surface connected at once you can greatly extend the usefulness of Reason. Here are a couple of examples.

The most obvious application for the Remote system is to have several people playing the same Reason system off the same computer at the same time. With several USB keyboards connected, or several MIDI keyboards via an interface, or a mixture of the two systems, you can share the same project. By locking each device to a module you can all have independent control over playing your own instruments in realtime. This is particularly interesting if you are using Combinator patches with sequencers inside them. As Reason outputs usually to a single stereo out, the sum total of your performance can be put through a single stereo amp channel.

Figure 2.18
An example of a realtime MIDI control surface

Another interesting application would be to have a controller locked to the mixer, and a keyboard then playing whatever you point it at. In this way you can have control over the mix of a project including solo and mute, pan , levels and effects settings as it is playing and as you are playing along with it.

You can mix and match these ideas to have, say, control over the mixer and several instruments yourself, but with further people playing other instruments from the same project.

If you discover that the auto-mapping isn't quite to your taste, or you have a more generic MIDI controller keyboard, you can re-map controls easily. By selecting Options > Remote Override Edit Mode you can choose a module in the rack to map. The modules are greyed out, and coloured symbols denote the parameters that can be mapped. If you double-click on a parameter it displays a lightning bolt. When you move a controller

Figure 2.19
Remote Override Edit mode

on your keyboard, or press a note, Reason maps that note or switch to the parameter you have selected.

If you control + click or right-click on a parameter in this mode, a separate window appears to let you choose specifically which

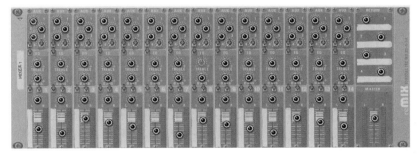

controller device should be used, and which type of control message should be read. By clicking the Learn button here you can see precisely what type of control you are pressing or turning on your keyboard. Once a control has been mapped, this window will also let you edit that mapping.

Figure 2.20
Keyboard Control mode

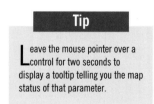

Leave the mouse pointer over a control for two seconds to display a tooltip telling you the map status of that parameter.

If you try to map the same key to two separate parameters, Reason will warn you of the fact and you will have to choose one or the other.

Even keys on the keyboard can be used as triggers, although they work as on/off switches rather than variables. Mapping a key to a knob or slider and then pressing it will change values between zero and 100 per cent. So you could for example have part of a keyboard or even a dedicated keyboard with controls mapped simply to muting and enabling channels, switching effects on and off or bypassing devices entirely. There is an additional menu of extra, system-specific overrides that you can map independently by selecting Options > Additional Remote Overrides. These include undo / redo, auto-quantize, patch selection and so on. With a bit of planning and some sticky labels on your keys to remind you what they trigger, you can control almost every aspect of a Reason song in a live setting without ever touching the mouse.

In Remote Override Edit Mode, mapped parameters display as orange or yellow lightning bolts. Every other symbol represents an un-mapped parameter.

If you set up specific maps, say for a generic MIDI keyboard, they are saved with the song file. In order to be able to easily use them again and again it's a good idea to save them once as a template file, then open and save this under a new file name each time you start a project. Otherwise you may have to re-specify this custom mapping each time.

Sound locations

Reason 2.5

When you open a patch or file browser in Reason there are some special shortcut buttons available. The four folder buttons correspond to sound locations set in the preferences. It's good practice to keep your ReFills and samples properly organized in a few folders, or even just in one. In the Sound Locations preference page, you can set up to four locations that Reason will remember and the buttons in the file browser will jump you straight to those folders. This can save you a huge amount of time in wandering around your hard drive looking for files.

A good way to organize sounds might be to have one folder for ReFills, one for samples and one for your own patches. Hit the cross next to the location buttons to delete the links and specify a new one.

Reason 3

In Reason 3 the Sound Locations section is removed. This function is now incorporated into the new Browser. Folders and ReFills can be dragged into the Locations window in the Browser for quick access. You can also create Favourites lists in the Favourites section, adding as many patches and samples from different sources as you like. This is a great way to keep, say, all your hip hop sounds from different folders and ReFills in a single list for quick access. Being able to zap straight to pre-selected lists is handy when you're jamming live, or just feeling spontaneous. With Combi patches this is a great way of keeping entire performances or multi-instruments just one click away at all times.

Hip hop

A brief history of hip hop

Hip hop originated in New York in the early 1970s when DJs started to cut up beats and loops from soul and funk records. Soon after this began, MCs started to talk over the beats, and rapping developed quickly into an integral part of the genre. A key early player was DJ Kool Herc, who fused beats from reggae, dub and disco records together using an audio mixer, making him a pioneer of scratching and many of the techniques practised widely today.

It remained largely a live phenomenon until the development of the drum machine and later the digital sampler, which meant producers could start to manipulate and record beats and samples much more easily. Classic early drum sequencers like the Roland TR-808 formed the backbone of much of the hip hop produced in the 1980s, especially by pioneers like Afrika Bambaataa. The artificial sound produced by drum machines was considered a plus point rather than a problem as it gave the genre its own, instantly recognizable sound. In recent years, artists like The Beastie Boys have started using classic drum machines extensively again, particularly on their album To The Five Boroughs. The really crucial part of any hip hop track is the beat, almost always in 4/4, which has to drive the track.

The idea behind hip hop is to have a groove, and also to have attitude and provide the backing for a rapper. As such, a lot of hip hop has traditionally been made by sampling, programming drums and cutting up old records rather than recording a band in the conventional sense. In a lot of hip hop, achieving a lo-fi, gritty sound is the aim. This is especially true of heavyweights like The Wu-Tang Clan, who tend to use stripped-down and fairly jazzy, dischordant loops featuring samples of real instruments like pianos, organs and acoustic drums. Others like Public Enemy preferred soundscapes that were more dense and layered.

In the 1990s hip hop in America started to polarise. West coast hip hop, with artists like Dr Dre, Tupac and Snoop Dogg became characterised by a more polished, produced sound not entirely unlike R&B, eschewing sampling in favour of synths, session players and expensive production values. There are exceptions, like stalwart rap / rock crossover specialists Cypress Hill, with DJ Muggs and his unmistakable production style, and more recently, party favourites Ugly Duckling. The New York scene flourished too, with artists like Jay-Z, Nas, De La Soul and A Tribe Called Quest generally keeping things a bit more old school.

Today, hip hop is a huge global phenomenon, with artists in many countries producing their own take on the genre. French rapper MC Solaar and Latin group Orishas are fine examples of the way that hip hop has been adapted to incorporate very different cultures. Musically, a lot of innovation has come from the instrumental side of hip hop, from producers like DJ Shadow, RJD2 and bands like The Herbaliser.

Recommended listening

Jurassic 5 – *Jurassic 5* (1998)
Beastie Boys – *Licensed to Ill* (1986)
Public Enemy – *It Takes a Nation of Millions to Hold Us Back*   (1988)
Cypress Hill – *Black Sunday* (1993)
DJ Shadow – *Endtroducing* (1996)
De La Soul – *3 Feet High and Rising* (1989)
Dr Octagon – *Dr. Octagonecologyst* (1996)
Wu Tang Clan – *Enter the Wu-Tang (36 Chambers)* (1993)

The workshop

1 Getting started

Hip hop tracks tend to be between 80 and 100 BPM depending on the effect you're going for. Open a new Reason project and save it somewhere sensible. Create a 14:2 Mixer and set the project tempo to 85 BPM. The time signature should be 4/4. A beat is always a good place to start as it gives you a solid foundation to build the track on. You can use a Dr.REX for some preconstructed loops, but let's start with a ReDrum and build something a bit more unique to start with. Select some empty space in the rack and create a ReDrum. Click on the file button and navigate to the Reason Factory soundbank, and then the ReDrum Kits / Hip Hop Kits folder.

Figure 3.1
Locating a hip hop kit in the Browser

2 Choosing a kit

Remember that you can audition any patch via a MIDI keyboard from the
Browser. This is great because it means you don't have to load a patch to see
whether it's suitable or not. Kit number 2 has a good lo-fi sound to it so load
it up. Set the left and right markers so they cover an eight-bar loop. Say,
between bars 17 and 25. The reason for starting the drums a bit later is so
that you can create an intro and not have to shuffle the entire song back.
Activate the click and Loop buttons and hit record. A typical hip hop drumbeat is fairly straightforward, with a bit of a swing to it, mainly consisting of
bass drum, snare and hi-hat. The chances are your playing will be slightly out,
so open the Drum Lane editor to correct the notes.

Figure 3.2
An example of how a typical hip hop
beat might look in the Drum Edit view

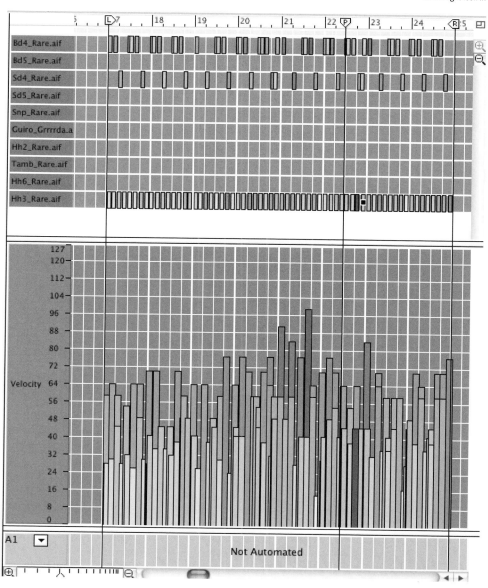

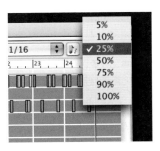

Figure 3.3
Set the strength of the quantize. Lower for a looser feel, higher for a tighter feel

File stage 1

Info

See page 4 for an explanation of the referencing used in these workshops.

3 Getting a feel

As you can see in the example, the snare beat hits every second and fourth beat and the hi hats play eight beats per bar. The bass drum punctuates the spaces between the snare but they never play at the same time. This is a text-book hip hop beat. At this point you could quantize all the notes, but even with a quantize value of 1/16 you'll find the beats lose all their natural feeling and start to sound too mechanical. You have two options. The first is to use the Quantize Amount menu at the top right of the screen. If you select all the notes, choose a value of 25% in this menu and then hit return, the notes will be pulled loosely into time. You should find the timing is tighter but still has a good swing to it.

Alternatively you can select individual notes or groups of notes and quantize them by different amounts. For example, The hi hats might need to be tight but the bass drum more loose. In this case, draw around the hi hats and quantize them using a snap value of 75%. Do the same with the bass drum notes but use a value of 25% to preserve the groove.

4 Enhancing the beat

Go back to the sequencer view and group the notes by drawing around them and selecting Edit > Group. Then use copy and paste to duplicate the loop a few times. Extend your right marker to fit the new loop. Now you're going to add some hits to the beat. Create an NN-19 sampler and click on the sample load button – that's the one in the centre, not on the left. Navigate to AMG ReFills > Norman Cook > Samples and load the Cook Stab 071 sample.

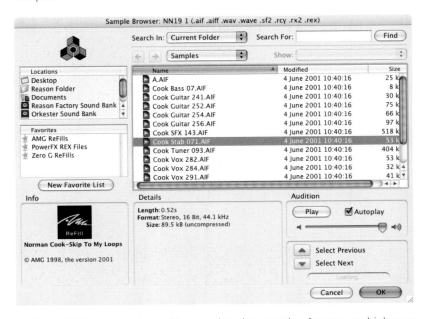

Figure 3.4
Loading sampled hits as one-shots into the sampler

Your MIDI keyboard should now play the sample. As you go higher or lower the sample will change in pitch. A common trick in hip hop is to match up stabs or hits with elements of the beat. You could try to play the hit over the drums, but here's how it's done quickly in Reason. Alt + drag a copy of the drum part onto the NN-19's sequencer track, or use copy and paste to do the same. It sounds pretty strange at first, so go into the Edit lane for the sampler. You can see the notes have been duplicated, but there are now too many of them and they're at the wrong pitch. What you want to do is match the stab with the bass drum and alter its pitch.

Figure 3.5
Quickly match a hit up with a beat by copying sequencer data between devices' tracks

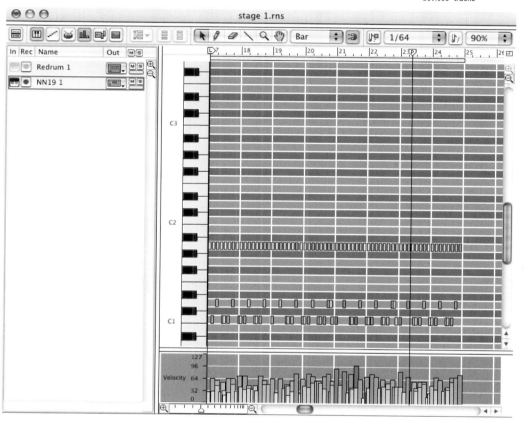

5 Vary the velocity

Delete the hi hat and snare notes on the sampler track, leaving just those copied from the bass drum track. The first step is to even out their velocities. In the velocity lane, choose the Pen tool or Line tool and draw a line across the bars so they even out. You can use the Pen or pointer to alter them individually to create some more variation if you like.

Figure 3.6
Achieve even velocities with the Line tool in the Velocity lane

Draw around the notes and drag them all higher up the keyboard, say to the A two octaves above middle C. Playing back, it sounds a bit better, but it still needs work. Try making the first hit of each bar longer by dragging its MIDI note out to the right. Set the snap value to 1/16 to enable more precise dragging. For more variation, try dragging the last two notes of each bar up a semitone.

6 Fatten up the drums

Back in Arrange mode, you could try rolling a little of the top end off the stab so it's less intrusive. Do this using the Filter Frequency control on the sampler. Taking it to a value of about 105 sounds good. Now select the ReDrum and choose Create > Scream 4 Distortion. Select the Tape preset and use the Cut section to boost the bass and mid a little. This gives the drums a warm, saturated tape sound that goes well with this kind of music.

Figure 3.7
The Scream 4 can be used to 'warm up' sounds as well as to distort them

Add an RV7000 Reverb unit to the sampler in the same way and load up a preset. CL Small Hall works well with a dry/wet setting of about 60. Remember you can preview patches from the Browser. When adding insert effects like this it often helps to solo up the module you're effecting so you can hear it in isolation. Choose a reverb that you like. You could have a heavy one or a very short one depending on how you see the track shaping up.

Figure 3.8
The RV-7000 reverb is perfect for adding a little space to your mix

7 Percussive piano

Let's add an intro, but one that can form a part of the track too. A very simple piano line could do this. Go back to the start of the track and create an NN-XT sampler. Load up a preset like the OldGrand from the Reason Factory sound bank. It may help at this stage to set the root key of the stab sample up to C sharp 3 to make the piano line easier to play.

Figure 3.9
Shifting the root note of a sample to make it fit the track

Activate the click and record a few bars of piano before the main beat comes in. Quantize and group this as before. Simple, repeated chords work much better here than anything fancy. Add a reverb to the piano sound – try the FilmScore preset with a dry / wet value of around 20. Also, add a compressor to the piano to give it some punch.

8 Scratch it up

Let's make the intro a bit more interesting. Load up a Dr.REX and navigate to Reason Factory Sound Bank – Dr.REX Instrument Loops > Scratch Loops. Most of these are a bit too manic for this track, but remember REX loops can be manipulated easily. Load up Scratch Beat 3_104. Use the Preview button on the Dr.REX module to see how the loop sounds at the new tempo. REX loops will automatically re-tempo themselves without changing pitch.

File stage 3

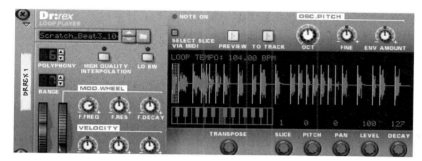

Figure 3.10
Auditioning REX loops

Set the left and right markers to loop over the start where there is currently only piano playing. Pressing the To Track button on the Dr.REX will put its data onto the track between those markers. An interesting trick is to double click some of the REX data to open it in the REX Edit lane. Once there you can start to rearrange it into your own pattern. Clicking on the Slice names on the left lets you preview each one, and by moving the slices around you can create infinite variations, or just take out or add the odd note. If you want a quick fix, select the notes and choose Edit > Change Events. Enter a value of around 50 in the Alter Notes box and have Reason randomise the pattern for you while keeping the timing intact. Repeat again with different alter values for the remaining bars if you like. This is a good way to avoid repetetiveness in your music, as it works with any sequencer data.

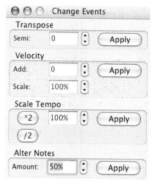

Figure 3.11
Use Alter Notes to introduce automatic variations

9 Copy and paste

You might want to start arranging the track a little bit now. Try alternating the stabs and the scratches so that they play four bars each at a time.

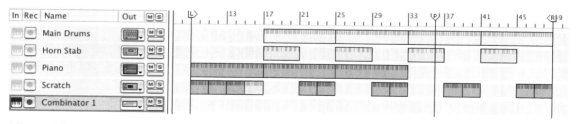

Figure 3.12
How the arrangement might look

After a while you could drop the piano out to stop it becoming annoying. Try loading up a Combinator, and loading the patch Player Hater Split from the Factory Sound Bank. This contains a really nice combo of a fat synth bassline and a great sounding lead. In fact the bassline fits really well so you could go back and record it over earlier parts of the track. Duplicate the Combi and use the second one just to play the lead line.

10 Drum edit

At this point it is a good idea to start introducing a bit of drum variation. For example, go to the point just before the lead line starts playing. It's good to have a fill or a small break to introduce a new instrument or theme. Enter the Drum Edit mode for the drum track and zoom in on the section right before the end of the bar. A good trick in hip hop is to have a repeated bass drum. It's a technique you can hear used extensively on DJ Shadow's album Endtroducing, and also Demon Days by Gorillaz. Delete all the drums from the second half of the last bar and then use the pen tool to draw some bass drum hits in as shown in Figure 3.13. Use the line tool to draw a velocity ramp so they fade in quickly.

Figure 3.13
Creating a velocity ramp in the Velocity Lane with the line tool

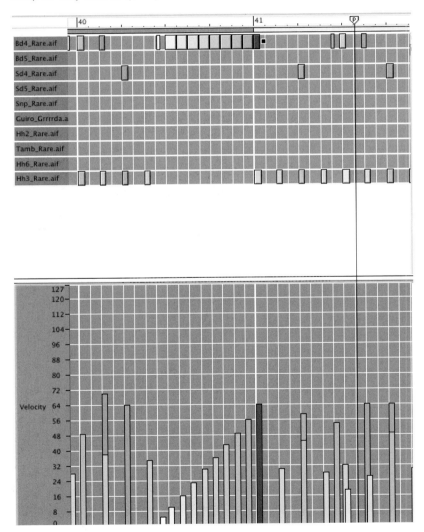

11 Break it down

Let's introduce a breakdown. Typically in hip hop these involve a bit of old school drum machinery. Go to the end of the arrangement you've made so far and load up a Dr.REX. There are some great REX files available for this, even better when you tweak them a bit. Try loading up AMG ReFills > Luke Cage 5.rx2. Press To Track to put it into the sequencer for eight bars or so. This loop sounds better if you transpose it a bit. This is easy to do with REX loops – just use the Transpose knob on the front panel of the loop player. Why not try automating a fader to make the loop die away just before it ends? As you play the new loop you've just introduced, hit record and grab the Filter Frequency slider on the loop player's front panel. As the loop gets towards the end, start to move the fader down to zero. Stop recording, play back and you should see the fader gains a green outline, meaning it's been automated. Enter Edit mode for the REX player and you can see the filter control ramp. If you like, you can re-draw it with the line tool to make it perfectly even. You could also have drawn it this way in the first place.

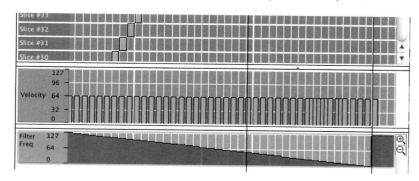

Figure 3.14
Automating Filter Frequency sliders in the Automation Lane.

12 To maximum effect

Try adding some reverb and a little compression to the new drum loop. Use effects as sends attached to the main mixer rather than directly to the REX player. Remember that when you have loaded a REX loop into a loop player it can be played in the same way as an instrument, slice by slice on a MIDI keyboard. You don't actually have to use the preset pattern at all. Copying a few bars of scratching over the break fills it out nicely. After a break it's always good to come back strongly, so bring everything back in straight after the loop dies away. Here's a good trick to help the transition between the break and the song coming back in again. Where the electronic loop is fading out because of its automated filter, do the same with another beat, only in reverse. Load up another REX player and find a good loop to use just once. Try AMG ReFills > Black II Black Vols 1&2 > Dope.REX. Blast it through a Scream 4 on the Tube preset to beef it up, and then Automate its filter as before, only this time starting at zero and going up to 100. If you enter Edit view for the new loop player you can activate its automation lane by clicking the Show Controller Lane

File stage 5

Figure 3.15
Show or hide Automation Lanes for any available parameter for a module.

Figure 3.16
Drawing ramps is the easiest way to achieve smooth automation

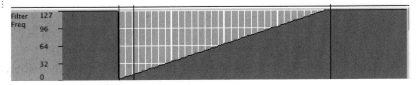

button at the top, and then choosing Filter Freq from the dropdown list. Then draw a ramp going from 0 to 100 for the duration of the loop. This is a great technique to try in many situations, as it lets you take two fairly simple loops and blend them dynamically to sound great.

13 Vocal samples

One technique that's used a lot in hip hop is to have very short vocal samples thrown in, usually stuttered with the beat. This is often done by a DJ scratching a record, but you can replicate it in Reason. Try this towards the end of the track, or over the start if you like. Create an NN-19 and load a sample using the middle file load button. Go to Zero G ReFills > Jungle Warfare > NN19 and select Scatter.wav. It is now playable from your MIDI keyboard. There's a slight gap at the start of the sample which makes it hard to play in sync, so on the sampler, use the Sample Start knob to adjust it so that the voice starts the instant you press the key, with no delay. A setting of about 20 seems to work. The vocal sample gets more depth and sits better in the mix if you add a small amount of delay with a DDL-1 attached as an insert and the dry / wet set to about 7.

File stage 6

Figure 3.17
Use the NN-19's Sample Start knob to tailor pre-recorded samples

14 Change events

The break still sounds a little bit empty so try putting an instrumental loop over it. Create a new REX player and try Factory Sound bank > Dr.REX Instrument Loops > Gtrwah_098_Chronic. To keep it interesting, use the Change Events trick you learned earlier on to modify some of the groups. In fact this loop works pretty well so try pasting a few instances of it in after the break as well. To finish the break off, try copying in the repeated bass drum notes that you created in step 10. Paste it as before, right at the end of the bar.

Figure 3.18
This is how your arrangement might look

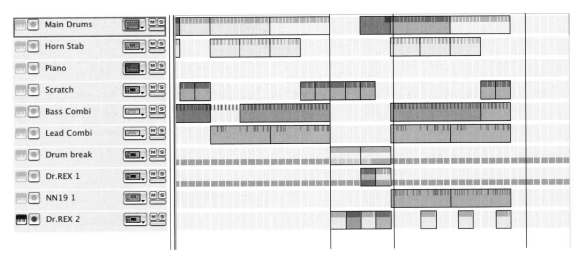

15 Sub bass beats

Another trick in hip hop is to throw in a few sub bass sounds on top of the beats to keep things interesting and give the track more depth. You can do this with a ReDrum, but as you'll probably only want to use a single sample, an NN-19 will do just as well. There's a good sample in the Factory Sound Bank > ReDrum Kits > Sorted Drums > Bass Drums folder called Bd7_Rare. Boost it through a compressor to bring its level up a bit, as it's fairly quiet to start with. It works best played immediately between the first and second beats of a bar, complementing the original bass drum. This is used quite a lot on hip hop records. You can get away with recording a couple of bars, quantizing, grouping and then just copying and pasting for the rest of the track. Use it sparingly or it becomes annoying.

File stage 7

Figure 3.19
Adding a compressed sub bass drum

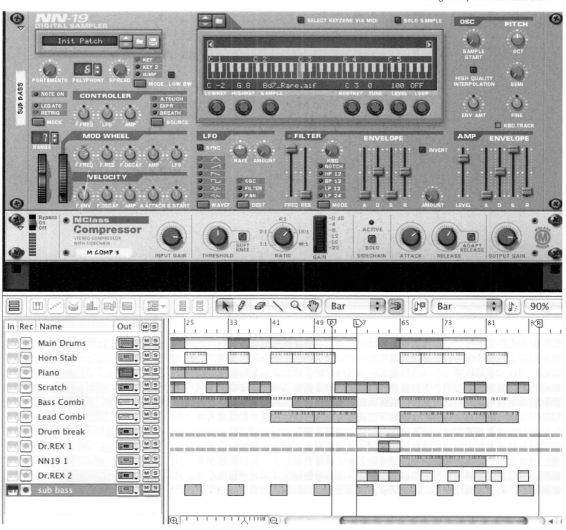

16 Crackling background

Figure 3.20
Adding record crackle to a track

Another technique that's used extensively in hip hop is to make the track sound like it's been played off a vinyl record, even if it hasn't. The most common way to do this is to add a sample of record crackle and loop it throughout the track. This can be done by creating an NN-19 and loading the sample called Fx2_CutCodes.wav from the Drum Kits > xclusive drums > FX folder of the Factory Sound Bank.

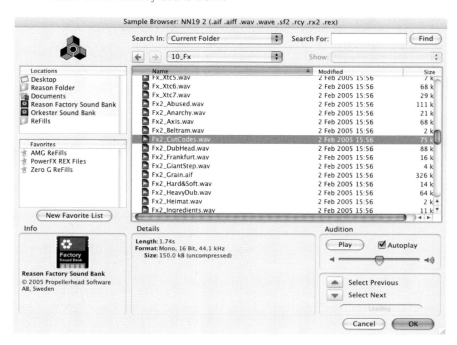

It's a short sample, so rather than pasting in hundreds of MIDI notes to keep triggering it, just set the Loop of the sample to FW using the front panel of the sampler. By placing one note at the start of the track, the crackle will then play for the duration of the track.

Figure 3.21
Setting the Loop mode of a sample so it plays indefinitely

Having said that, if you start playback from anywhere other than the beginning of the track you won't hear the crackle, as it won't have been triggered. To avoid this you can add a note every few bars if you like. The net effect will be the same, it will just make it easier to hear the crackle as you zoom around and audition the track from different places.

17 Master mix

Your arrangement should hopefully be well on its way by now and you might be ready to start thinking about a mix. Add a Mastering Combi between the Hardware Interface at the top of the rack, and the Mixer. This will pass the whole mix through the processor. It's worth doing this before you start to mix, as adding it will change the characteristics of any mixing you've already done and you may have to alter it anyway. The hip hop preset is a good place to start.

Figure 3.22
Preset Mastering Combi patches

Adding the Mastering Combi, you'll probably find that the snare suddenly jumps out at you a bit too much, so go back to the ReDrum and take it down a little. The drums need a bit of a boost in the mid range so attach a PEQ2 to the ReDrum and tweak it so that the mid is brought out a bit more.

Figure 3.23
Tweaking the EQ of a device using a PEQ-2

Use the various EQ band controls on the Equalizer that's part of the Combi to even out the track a bit. Initially it's a bit too bass heavy. The bassline benefits from the addition of a little reverb via the Aux 1 send, or wherever you have attached a reverb as an insert on the desk. If the bass is too buzzy, go into the Bass Combi and locate the Line Mixer that's submixing the signals. Use the channel 1 gain knob to lower the level of the buzzy synth, leaving more of the warmer one. This will smooth the sound out a little.

Figure 3.24
Editing a Combi patch from within the Combinator

18 Hip hop blend

File stage 10

The scratching should probably sit fairly low in the mix, behind the beats. The sub bass can overwhelm things so control it by keeping it relatively low and also compressing it and rolling off a little of the bottom end using the mixer's EQ. The drum break beat on channel 7 might need a bit more treble adding to it, as since the addition of the mastering effects it has become quite bass-heavy. The vocal sample on channel 9 also needs boosting a bit to compete with the rest of the mix. The horn stab that's synchronised with the bass drum should blend with the beat, as if it were a part of the drum kit. The piano line should be clear and piercing, as should the lead synth line.

Drum'n'bass

A brief history of drum'n'bass

A relative newcomer to the global scene, drum'n'bass is also sometimes called jungle music. Although views differ on precise terminology, they both refer essentially to the same kind of music. The term jungle was around first, when the music was only found in clubs, and before it had made the leap to mainstream success. As it grew in prominence the name drum'n'bass appeared, and is now generally used to mean the more commercial varieties, and Jungle the more underground.

Emerging from the rave and acid house scenes of the early 1990s, drum'n'bass tends to concentrate, as the name suggests, on breakbeats and huge basslines. Production and arrangements are relatively sparse, the rapid-fire beats and huge electronic basses doing most of the work. Beats were originally sped-up hip hop and funk breaks, and the bass lines borrowed heavily from dub and reggae. As the genre developed it started to incorporate MCs and rappers performing freestyles over it.

Early stars of drum'n'bass include A Guy Called Gerald, Goldie and Mickey Finn. As its distinctive sound and fast tempo started to make an impression on the wider music scene, people began to take it in different directions in an attempt to achieve more commercial success. This more accessible form of drum'n'bass, pioneered by artists like LTJ Bukem and 4Hero held on to the fast breakbeats but swapped menacing synths and basses for an altogether friendlier approach. With more of a jazz influence, this 'intelligent' drum'n'bass was altogether warmer and more atmospheric. Later, Roni Size and Reprazent would gain a lot of critical acclaim, even winning the Mercury Music Prize in 1997 for *New Forms*, an album which managed to sound 'underground' and yet appeal to a wide audience with its heavy use of jazz double bass. Other bands like Red Snapper also advocated a more live approach to the genre.

Today the genre is incredibly diverse. Artists like Ed Rush and Optical make techstep, leading DJ Fabio produces Liquid Funk music, and Drumfunk has also enjoyed a renaissance. On a wider scale, whilst drum'n'bass has largely disappeared from the charts it maintains a healthy presence in clubs. One of its enduring strengths is that being largely synth and sample based, it isn't too difficult to get involved in writing and producing it on a laptop or in a home studio. With such attention paid to the drums and the bass, a bit of innovation in drum programming and a decent sound system to fully appreciate the bass are essential.

Recommended listening

Roni Size & Reprazent – *New Forms* (1997)
A Guy Called Gerald – *28 Gun Bad Boy* (1992)
Peshay – *Miles From Home* (1999)
Red Snapper – *Making Bones* (1998)
LTJ Bukem – *Journey Inwards* (2000)
Ed Rush – *Mad Different Methods* (1996)
Squarepusher – *Hard Normal Daddy* (1997)

The Workshop

1 Getting started

Drum'n'bass generally operates at a tempo of between 160 and 180 BPM and tends to be more syncopated that the electronic styles out of which it grew. A sensible place to start is with a beat, as here more than most styles, it forms the essence of the track. There are many fine REX files in the drum'n'bass style, and you can speed up hip hop beats to achieve the same effect, but where you can it's better to create original beats. Create a new project, add a mixer and set the tempo to 160BPM, or something similar if you prefer it a little slower or faster. Load up a ReDrum and activate the click. What you're going to do is come up with a beat for the intro to the track. Playing beats this fast by hand is tricky so here's a good time to use the ReDrum's excellent pattern and step sequencing features. Click on the patch load button and navigate to the Factory Sound Bank > DrumNBass Kits folder. Audition some of the patches – Kit 01 works well for an intro.

Figure 4.1
Loading up a drum'n'bass kit

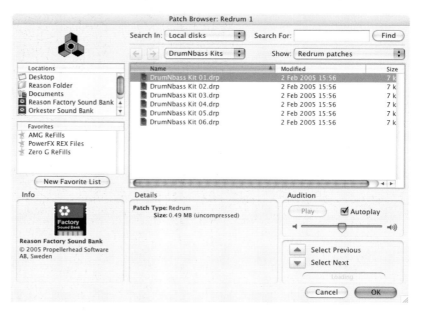

2 Tweak the drums

The bass drum is quite high pitched so you may want to lower it a little using the Pitch knob on drum channel 1 on the ReDrum.

You can start to customise the kit to see if other drum hits would work better. For example channel 9 contains a hi hat but it's a bit thin. Right click or control+click on the name of the sample (in red) and you can select another sample from the sound library. Just the sample is replaced, not the whole kit. You can also use the file load button or the up/down arrows on each channel to do the same. Here's a great tip for playing the beats in – if it's too hard to play them live at the full tempo, just drop the project tempo temporarily, record them and then take it back up again. Key to getting a good hi hat sound is using two slightly different hi hats in different drum channels. That way, you avoid the mechanical sound of an unchanging cymbal. The bass drum has a lot of tail on it, so use the Length knob on its channel on the ReDrum to tighten it up. A Length setting of 49 seems to work well. Quantizing the beat to 1/16 tightens it up and irons out any variations.

Figure 4.2 (left)
Editing elements of a kit from the front panel of the ReDrum

Figure 4.3
Edit Length and Pitch until the kit sounds right

3 Big drum sound

Enter Drum Edit mode for the track and, zooming in, iron out any major inconsistencies in the velocities of the notes. Be sure to leave some in to maintain a natural feel, but nothing too quiet or too unnaturally loud.

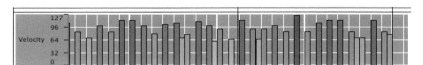

Figure 4.4
Some naturally occurring variation in velocity is good

Use the pitch, length and volume controls for each of the drum channels on the ReDrum to get the sound you want. With the pattern sorted, beef up the sound a bit. Try adding a Scream 4 as an insert, perhaps with the Overdrive preset used but the Damage setting dropped a little lower than usual – say, to around 45. Try also adding an RV7000 reverb, and find a preset. The Mid Hall preset fits quite well if you drop the decay right down and the dry/wet down to about 23.

Figure 4.5
Adding reverb to the drums

Figure 4.6
Alter the sound of REX loops with the filter frequency slider

Now let's create another percussion line to go with the beat, in order to start building it up. Add a Dr.REX and load up a file – try ZeroG ReFills > Jungle Warfare Demo > Jazz Ridez.rx2. This is a cool break but for the moment it would be better without the bass end, as you're building up to introducing the big drums later on. Use the filter control on the Dr.REX to roll it off. Set the filter mode to BP12 and play with the frequency slider until you're happy with it. To make up for stripping out some of the bass you can whack the new loop through a compressor.

File stage 2

4 On a roll

Here's a good trick for programming drum'n'bass beats. A common technique is to repeat hits very quickly but only for a very short time, and to keep doing this at different points with different drum sounds. In fact you will hear this on almost any drum'n'bass record. Give it a go. Repeat the groups of notes you've created so far and solo up the ReDrum. Find a point in a bar where a break would sound good and enter Edit mode. Try it first with the snare. Zoom in and set the snap value to 1/64. This is so you can get loads of notes in really close to one another. If you drag the beat you have chosen down to its smallest size, select it and then use copy and paste, Reason will automatically place an identical note immediately after it. Keep pasting until the notes reach the start of the next bar, as seen in Figure 4.7. Use the Line tool to draw a velocity ramp so that they fade in very quickly.

Figure 4.7
Creating very rapid drum fills

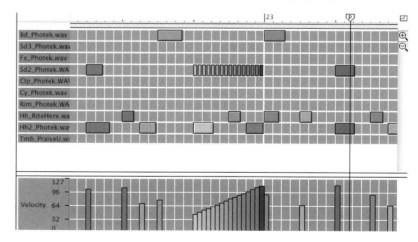

Locate another likely spot and try the same with the bass drum. In drum'n'bass you can throw these fills in pretty much anywhere and they sound good. When and where you use them is up to you but applied liberally, they keep things interesting. Finally add another REX player and load a tambourine loop from the Factory Sound Bank's REX percussion loops folder. This is easier than trying to make a ReDrum do a convincing fast tambourine, especially with this style of music. Stick it through some reverb and play with the pitch control on the Dr.REX until you're happy that the sound sits in the mix.

Figure 4.8
Things are starting to get busy

5 Big bottom bass

Now try adding some bass. Along with the drums, this will form the backbone of the track. Load up a Subtractor and choose the Factory Sound Bank Garage Bass 1 patch.

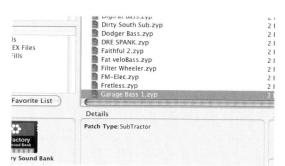

Figure 4.9
Loading a bass patch

Play with the synth's controls a bit to try to beef up the patch. Don't be afraid to try throwing a Scream 4 on too, maybe with the overdrive preset, but used sparingly.

File stage 3

Copy and paste a few bars of what you have. Now, let's bring in the main body of the track. Here's a tip – try dropping the drums out for a few beats before the main drum, which you're about to create, comes in. Load up a Dr.REX and call up the AMG 160db ReFill, Break 322.rx2. This is a classic drum'n'bass loop.

Figure 4.10
Locating a REX loop

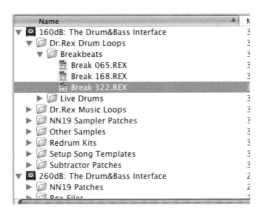

Copy the loop to the track using the To Track button on the Dr.REX and attach a Maximizer or a compressor to it to give it some grunt. The loop already has reverb recorded on it so there's probably no need to add any. Rather than copying the previous bassline, let's create a new one. Create an NN-XT sampler and load the Upright+Harm patch from the Factory Sound bank. This patch has samples layered by velocity, so the harder or softer you play the MIDI notes, the different the sample you will get. Try it – playing softly plays the normal note, but hitting a key hard produces a slide or bent note. With a double bass this sounds great. Try playing in a new bassline – something simple but a bit jazzy. Here's a tip – by editing the velocities of a velocity-sensitive patch like this in the key editor, you can control what sounds are triggered, as well as just how hard it sounds. Repeat this new section for a few bars, and then repeat the step from earlier in step 4 where you created very fast fills. You can do it with any hits, even the tambourines. REX files can be made to repeat like this just as easily as regular MIDI notes. You just have to identify which slices you want to repeat. Try repeating several in succession. A lot of the interest in drum'n'bass comes from the seemingly random assault of fills, breaks and samples. The most extreme example of this is someone like Squarepusher. When you layer up drum parts in drum'n'bass you tend to find that you get all kinds of unexpected, complex but great-sounding results from the convergence of all the different beats (Figure 4.11).

Another good way of randomizing a pattern and especially a REX loop is to select the group of notes and choose Edit > Change Events. Use the Alter Notes field to enter an amount of randomization and hit Apply. Voila – instant variation! This is a great timesaver in drum'n'bass where the beats are very organic and keep changing most of the time.

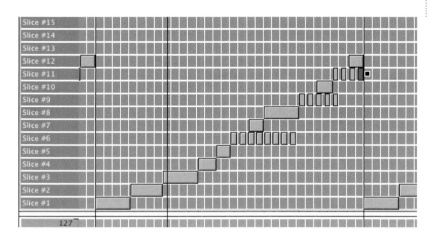

Figure 4.11
Editing and re-ordering REX patterns in the REX Edit Lane

6 Break it down

Now try winding it down a notch or two. Create an NN-19 and open Zero G ReFills > Jungle Warfare > NN19 > Rhodes Chord LP2. Play in some simple notes. To equalize their velocities, go to the velocity lane for the NN-19 and use the line tool to smooth them out. You may want to stagger some of them in, as shown in Figure 4.12.

File stage 4

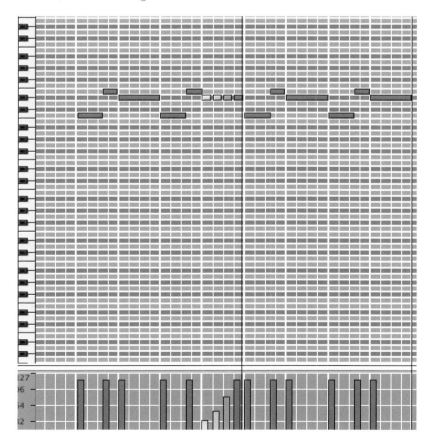

Figure 4.12
Adding a Rhodes line

Try fading the Rhodes chords out towards the end of the loop by automating the filter from full down to zero as it ends. This process is described in more detail in the previous chapter. Try adding a little delay to the NN-19. Create a ReDrum and load up some samples into its various channels. Remember that you can load any sample into a ReDrum, not just drums. Look in the ReFills and find some. See if they fit and if they do, throw a couple on over the break to make it a bit more atmospheric. Then copy in the main theme so that it comes straight back in after the break. Try switching back to the synth bass for a few bars as well. Only this time, you're going to sequence the notes with a Matrix. This will give you some more interesting patterns.

7 What is the Matrix?

Select the Subtractor you created earlier and select Create > Matrix Pattern Sequencer. You can play the Matrix independently of the main sequencer to build up your pattern. Pressing Run on the Matrix, you should hear a repeated bass note. Switch the Resolution knob down to 1/8 to keep it sensible, and move the octave button down to 1. Now you can draw in a pattern and the Matrix will play the synth. If you increase the Steps to 32 you get a longer pattern to play with. In fact you can use up to four banks of eight patterns in a single Matrix.

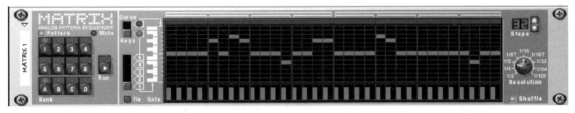

Figure 4.13
The useful Matrix pattern sequencer

With the Matrix selected and the left and right markers set where you want them, select Edit > Convert Pattern Track to Notes. Now you can drag these new notes to the Subtractor's sequencer track and delete the Matrix, or disconnect it temporarily if you like.

8 Combi patches

File stage 5

As well as evolving beats and drums, drum'n'bass often has some dark synth sounds and samples chucked in as well. Browse around the ReFills by selecting Create > Create Device by Browsing Patches. Search for a patch called Overdub, which works well here. There's a Combinator patch called Modular Madness in the Factory Sound Bank that's full of cool sounds with which to punctuate the track. Give it a try, especially earlier on in the track. Many of the rhythmic and Synth Effect Combi patches work well with drum'n'bass. The great thing about Combi patches is that they sync automatically to the tempo of the track.

Figure 4.14
Combi patches

9 Bridge the gaps

The transitions between the loud and quiet sections of the track are a bit dry at the moment. That is, everything stops dead. Sometimes this may be what you're after, but in other cases it's good to have something to smooth over the join. This can be as simple as adding a reverb or delay to the tail end of a drum or instrument loop. If this was audio you could apply an effect just to one clip, but it's MIDI, so you have to add an effect to the track. Doing this will add the effect to the whole track, but you only want one small section of it to be effected. The way around this is to simply duplicate the module in question, create a new sequencer track for it and copy only the group of notes for that bar to the new track. Remember to delete the original group of notes so you don't have two playing at the same time. In this case, duplicate the Dr.REX that's playing the main beat. If you hold down Shift as you paste it, it will be auto-routed into a free mixer channel.

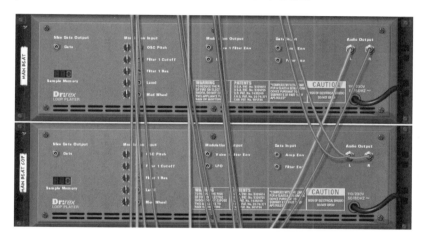

Figure 4.15
Duplicating modules in the rack

Add a delay unit as an insert to the duplicated Dr.REX. A dry/wet mix of about 50 works well. Copy the relevant notes and delete the originals. You should find that the copied drum part now delays nicely into the break. You can use this technique at other points in the track – just drag the data from the original track to the copied one which has effects attached.

10 Messing with samples

You should have something resembling a good arrangement by now. How exactly you have built the track will depend on your own preference, but you will probably have an intro / build-up / main theme / break / main theme / outro, as can be seen in the file Stage 6. One final interesting thing for the track arrangement might be to go back through and throw in a few reversed samples. This is a good way of squeezing some more life out of your existing samples, and works well in drum'n'bass where weird sounds and hits aren't uncommon. There are two ways to do this. The first is to load up a sample in an NN-XT and set the Play Mode knob to BW, for backwards.

File stage 6

Figure 4.16
Altering Loop mode on the NN-XT

The second is to use the RV7000's reverse effects. Create a Subtractor and load up a lead patch. Then attach an RV7000, open its Remote Programmer window and set the algorithm to Reverse. Now when you play the synth the sound is reversed. Try switching on Tempo Sync too, and adding a Scream 4, maybe with the Fuzz preset. This is an interesting technique to try with anything dark and atmospheric. It works just as well on pianos, drums or any other sound source.

Figure 4.17
RV-7000 Reverse effect

File stage 7

Figure 4.18
Adding a Mastering Combi

11 Mix it up

Now try mixing the track. The first thing to do, before you set any final levels, is to add a mastering Combi between the mixer and the hardware interface. This ensures that the stereo output of the whole mixer, and therefore the whole track, will pass through the Combi.

As a good starting point, try the Bass&Drum.cmp preset. You should notice that it immediately makes the track sound bigger and punchier. Now go through the mixer channels and EQ and set faders based on what sounds good to you. There are three different basslines and multiple drum tracks in this arrangement, so it's important to balance them all out. Solo up tracks to hear them better, but remember that what sounds good on its own won't always sound good in the mix, and it's the mix that really counts. It can be a good idea at this stage to add a reverb and a compressor to the mixer as send

Figure 4.19
Adding send effects

Figure 4.20
The channel strip

effects, and then use the Aux knobs on the mixer to add subtle amounts of each to a channel if and when it needs it. The send effects can have their master level controlled by using the Return section at the top right of the mixer.

As not every element plays through the whole track, it's usually a good idea to set up a loop round the bit you're working on. The synth bass is pretty heavy so you could try reining it in slightly by rolling off just a touch of the bass EQ on the mixer. The double bass on channel 6 is fairly huge too, so add a little reverb and back the fader off slightly. The Subtractor created in stage 10 is very bassy so use the EQ on its mixer channel to boost the treble a bit and take out some of the bottom end.

The Main Beat (on channel 5 in the tutorial file) should be distinct from the bass. The basses are very low and fat, and the beats much higher in pitch. Even their bass drums aren't very bassy. They exist mainly in the mid and treble. This is typical of drum'n'bass, and lets the drums skitter around on top of the thumping basslines. The drums should sound really punchy and the basses should thunder, but not distort or drown out anything else. The other elements like the samples and the synths are more mid-range, and so shouldn't be too hard to mix in with the bass and drums. The main beats can benefit from some spacey reverbs, if they don't already have some on them. Other elements are generally more dry, with just enough reverb to make them sit in the mix. Drum'n'bass tends to have a fairly pumped, compressed sound to it, but this doesn't mean you should overuse compression, just use it in the right places.

Dub

A brief history of dub

Originated in Jamaica in the early 1970s, dub is not entirely unlike reggae music. But where the latter is more structured and song-based, dub tends to be much more about the sound and groove of the music than any kind of traditional song structure. In fact a lot of dub has no vocals in the conventional sense, just snippets thrown in and typically drenched in delay for maximum effect. The most important elements of dub are the bass and drums, followed by the percussive elements like guitars or pianos, and finally the many sound effects scattered through a track to build on the underlying riff or groove. The short, choppy guitar and piano hits often play the second and fourth beats of the bar, as that's where dub tends to place the emphasis. The timing is also usually fairly loose with a great deal of swing rather than any rigid, mechanical adherence to a metronome.

The most easily identifiable dub trick is a one shot snare hit that echoes off, losing bass and mid range as it finally disappears into the mix. Usually these are only loosely synchronized with the tempo of the track. In fact, the beats picking up the track as the delayed drum fill or hit rattles off into the distance is probably one of the most heavily used devices in dub. The extensive use of this certain type of delay effect can be traced back to early dub producers' fondness for the Roland Space Echo delay unit.

Dub is very bass heavy, and the basses are fat and round. This is partly due to the fact that it started off as a type of music that was mainly played on local sound systems in Jamaica, where bass could really be felt. Early pioneers include King Tubby, who along with Lee Scratch Perry is widely credited with inventing dub. Pure dub is produced mainly using real instruments – guitars, drums, pianos and vintage keyboards, and mixes tend to be relatively sparse. Tracks might be five or six minutes long and meander around rather than having a verse/chorus structure or building up to any kind of crescendo.

In the 1990s dub started to exert more of an influence on a wide range of musical styles. The Mad Professor and Scientist are two leading exponents of dub in the UK, and you can hear definite veins of dub running through selected works of bands like Massive Attack, Underworld, Primal Scream, The Orb and producers like Adrian Sherwood. Dub itself has diversified too, at one extreme morphing into the harder-edged Dancehall of artists like Buju Banton, and at the other, the almost ambient electronic dub of Kruder & Dorfmeister, and the more upbeat electronic dub of Tosca.

Recommended listening

King Tubby – *Rastafari Dub* (1974-1979)
Augustus Pablo – *Earth's Rightful Ruler* (1983)
Mad Professor – *The African Connection* (1983)
Lee 'Scratch' Perry – *Arkology* (1997)
Prince Far I – *Voice of Thunder* (1981)
Richard Dorfmeister – *A Different Drummer Selection* (2003)
Massive Attack Vs. Mad Professor – *No Protection* (1995)

The Workshop

1 Slow it down

Dub tends to be fairly laid back compared to other styles. The project file in the dub folder is at 75 BPM. You can alter it up or down if you like but this is a fairly solid speed for this type of music. Let's start with the main beat. Dub tracks often start with a short delayed drum fill, but you can add that a little later when there's a theme for it to lead into. Load up a Dr.REX player and navigate to the powerFX ReFill folder. From there, load the REX file called 080Nagual_Drums_03. This is a good introductory dub beat, and as it's a REX file it'll easily stretch down slightly to the project tempo.

Figure 5.1
Loading REX loops

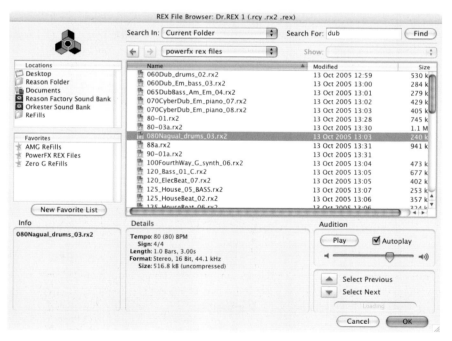

Scroll into the project a little to give you room to add an intro later. Then set up a loop and use the To Track button on the Dr.REX to place the beat into the sequencer.

2 Laid back beats

Now load up a ReDrum, as you'll need to create a main beat for when the track kicks in properly. There are three dub kits in the Factory Sound Bank > ReDrum Kits folder, so pick one that you like. Remember you can replace elements of the kit in a moment. In the example, kit 2 is loaded. It's good but the snare has delay pre-recorded, which isn't always what you want. Click on the name field in the ReDrum's channel 3 and you can quickly choose from a list of alternative snares. The sample called Monk works well.

Figure 5.2
Loading different parts of a drum kit

Traditional dub beats tend to be syncopated with a lot of swing. There's a fairly simple back and forth between the bass and snare, while the hi-hats carry everything along. It's really important to have at least a couple of hi hat samples to play, as one single one will sound too mechanical. In the project file, channels 8 and 9 have two suitably different sounds which you can play and will still sound organic. It's usually better to program dub beats by playing them live as it maintains the organic feel that you need. If you're doing more modern electronic dub, a Matrix would work just as well for a more computerised feel. Shift the loop up a bit so you're in clear space. Enable the click and record a beat. The pattern recorded in the project file is a good example of a shuffling dub beat.

3 Loose and lazy

Quantizing is usually necessary, but with this kind of beat it's better to enter Drum Edit mode and quantize the separate drum elements individually. The bass drum should be fairly tight, so you can draw around the bass drum notes and use a quantize value of 1/16 and a quantize percentage of 75% to pull them into time.

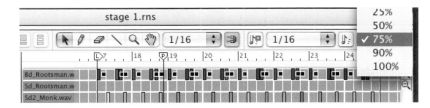

Figure 5.3
Setting the quantize amount

Repeat with the snare beats but use a quantize percentage of 50%. Then for the two hi hats, try using a value of 1/16 but a percentage of just 10%. The natural variations in velocity from your playing that you can see in Figure 5.4 actually work to your advantage as they more or less replicate the way that a real dub drummer would hit the hi hats slightly differently every time.

Figure 5.4
Don't worry about natural velocity fluctuations in dub

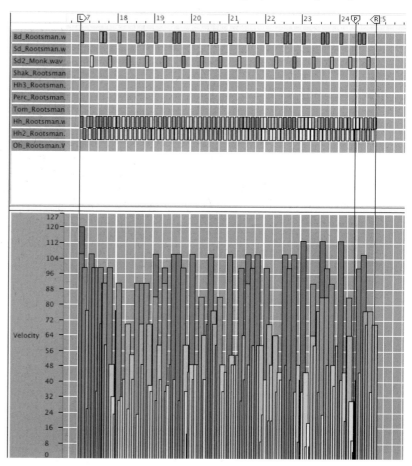

In dub you don't tend to effect entire kits unless you're going for something spacey. Here, the snare is quite dry so try adding a reverb as a send to the main mixer, then using the S1 control on channel 3 of the ReDrum to send the snare through some of that reverb. You can repeat this with the bass and hats if you like, but it works well for now to just effect the snare. You could also attach a compressor to the ReDrum, and use the level controls on the front panel to even out the elements of the kit. It's worth using the Length control on the bass drum to tighten it up, as it's a bit boomy at the moment. A setting of around 48 seems to work well (Figure 5.5).

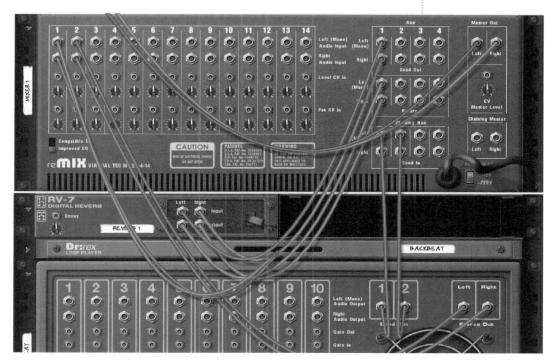

4 Big bass

Before going too much further you may want to create a bassline, as with the main beat it will form the backbone of the track and give you something to work with. Load up a Malstrom and navigate to the Factory Sound Bank > Malstrom > Basses folder. Choose the preset called Punchy Bass. Initially it's a bit too synth-sounding, but if you deactivate OSC B you lose the synth and are just left with the massive sub bass. dub basslines are fairly simple and often consist of repeated octaves or repeated triads, notes 1, 3 and 5 of a chord, as in this example. Be careful again with quantizing. In the example, values of 1/16 and 25% were enough to keep it tight without losing the groove. It is worth adding a compressor to the Malstrom to control the bass, which is fairly large and needs reining in a little. Now add a Dr.REX and load up a tambourine loop from the Factory Sound Bank. Copy it to the track as before and add a little reverb. This will help the rhythm flow better. The tambourine should sit low in the mix so as not to fight with the hi-hats. It should complement them but not overpower them.

Figure 5.5
A ReDrum connected to the mixer's send effects

File stage 3

Figure 5.6
A tambourine REX file – quick and easy

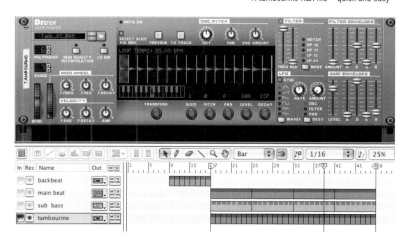

5. Adding a drum fill

Now go back and look at the intro. Currently it just contains a beat, so let's make it a bit more interesting. Move the playhead to just before the start of the first beats, and create an NN-XT sampler. Load up the patch called Dry Kit w Perc from the Factory Sound Bank > NN-XT > Drums > Drum Kits folder. You should find that by playing the bottom C, D and E flat in quick succession you get a very short drum roll consisting of a bass drum and two snares. Play this in just once, with the click track activated, right before the first beat. Quantize them if you like. At present it sounds a bit odd, but here's where it gets interesting. Attach an RV7000 to the NN-XT and load up the patch called EKO SpaceEcho1 from the sound bank. Based on how the delay sounds you may have to move the new notes a bit closer to the start of the other beat, so that the two cross over. You may also want to add a simple, short reverb to the new drum fill to give it a bit of depth.

Figure 5.7
Textbook dub echo with the RV-7000

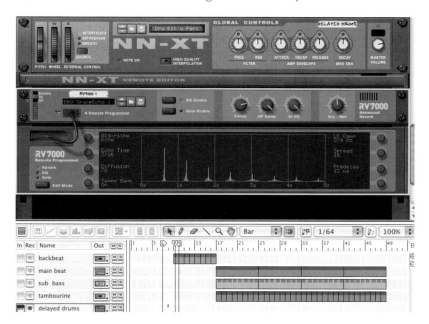

As it stands the intro is still fairly bare, so try loading up some samples to fill things out a bit. Create an NN-XT and load up some of the samples that you can find in Zero G ReFills > Koncept and Funktion > NN-19. If you hold shift to multiple select you can load all of them in at once. You then have to drag the key range bar for each sample to specify which notes you want to be able to use to trigger it. Otherwise every key will play an amalgamation of all the samples. You can edit any of the samples by selecting them in the NN-XT's editor window and using the fade in/out, tune, level and filter controls to get them just how you want them. This is a great way to submix a drum kit, for example, within a single NN-XT. It's also worth running the sampler through a delay unit to help everything blend together. You can audition samples in the NN-XT by holding the alt key and clicking on the name of the sample in the editor window.

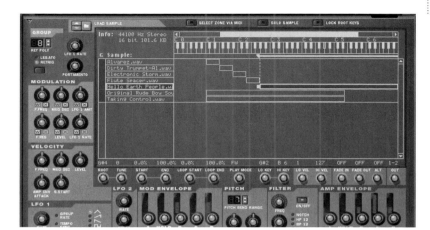

Figure 5.8
The NN-XT

6 Readymade sounds

The intro sounds good – don't be afraid to slap on some delays – so let's introduce a theme that can go over the introductory beats, and then lead into the main part of the track. Create a Combinator and load the patch Protection Grand from the factory sound bank > Piano folder. This is a fantastic timesaver, as this particular patch has a more or less ready-made dub piano sound, with some RV7000s ready set up and tempo synced. You can change the piano sound to something like B Grandpiano from within the Combi if you find the original piano sound a little too soft for this track.

File stage 5

Figure 5.9
Piano patches

Something really simple will do – often just two minor chords, as in the example. It's also worth deleting the last few notes of the intro beat here, to signify that a change in the track is about to happen. Leave a delayed snare hit to decay over the break.

The intro section is still lacking something. Go back to the NN-XT you created in step 5. Although only a few samples have been used so far, there are a lot more present in that patch. Usefully it's also running through the delay

Figure 5.10
Adding a shaker – keep it simple

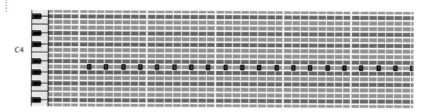

and reverb already, so it sounds great. As you play the intro section, record some drum and percussion hits. These work best on the second beat of a bar, as in the example. Loop it and keep recording, layering hits as you go. There's a rather nice shaker sample further up the keyboard in that NN-XT and if you play it every second and fourth beat of the bar, the delay gives it a fantastic live feel as it simulates you playing a real shaker (Figure 5.10).

7 Bongo beats

File stage 6

Now that the track is starting to take shape you could think about adding some variation later on to keep it moving. Load up a Dr.REX player and trying out some of the percussion loops in the AMG ReFIlls > Pukka Masala folder. They work quite well, thrown in just for a few bars. Try running it through a phaser to make it sound more interesting. Guitar is another good rhythmic element to use in dub tracks. Add another REX player and load the DubStrat REX loop from the Factory Sound Bank > music loops > variable tempo > downtempo folder. As it stands it's too busy but the beauty of REX loops is that you can mess about with them easily.

Figure 5.11
Viewing the slices of a
REX loop

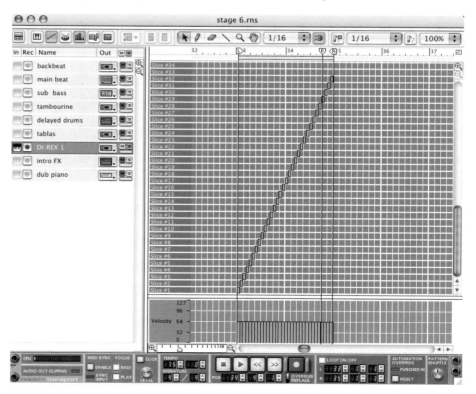

Locate a point a bit later on in the track and copy a bar of the guitar loop to the track. It will help you to solo up the guitar for a moment. Enter Edit mode and you can see the slices of the loop (Figure 5.11). By quickly double clicking on any group of notes you can jump directly to the Edit page for that module, which is a great timesaver.

The trick now is to delete most of the slices so you're left with a slower, more intermittent guitar part. Leave the second or second and fourth beats, but get rid of the rest. You should be left with something that looks like Figure 5.12

You might want to add a phaser to the guitar part by attaching one to the Dr.REX as an insert. If you do, set the feedback very low. Around 15 seems to work. Try bringing the piano part back in after a while. Feel free to throw in some more percussive hits over the rest of the track, as you did in step 6.

Figure 5.12
The REX loop after you have deleted most of the notes, leaving a simpler pattern

8 One hit wonders

If you look in the ReFill called Under Fire Future Funk in the AMG ReFills folder you'll find some great one-shot samples that you can throw in at strategic points to keep some variety going in the track. You might want to roll off some of the top end of these using EQ or just by lowering the filter frequency on the NN19 into which you have loaded them. Here's another tip – attach an RV7000 to each one and use the SpaceEcho 2 preset – it works brilliantly on these one-shot sounds. Leave the dry/wet control switched up to maximum for a really dense effect! If you are playing the notes in, play the key on the first beat of the bar. Because of the delay cause by the RV7000 you won't hear the sound until a fraction of a beat later, which sounds great.

File stage 7

Figure 5.13
The excellent SpaceEcho reverb preset

9 Horn of plenty

Figure 5.14
Editing the NN-XT's filters

Figure 5.15
Chaining multiple insert effects together

A fairly common type of instrument to use in dub is the trumpet, or a similar kind of horn sound. Probably the most realistic is the NN-XT patch called Three Trumpets on the Factory Sound Bank. Use the search field to find it – a handy tip for finding any patch by name or type rather than looking through folders. It's OK but not great, and will need a bit of work before it fits into the track without sounding false. The first thing to try is to add a little bit more hardness to the sound. The best way to do this is to use the Filter Frequency knob in the Velocity section on the NN-XT. Turn it higher to make the sound sharper, or lower to soften it. Make sure you've selected all samples within the NN-XT so they will all be altered.

Next try adding some reverb. Just a little, as you'll need to put some delay on too in a moment. The RV7000's FilmScore preset works well at a dry / wet setting of about 13. Next, add another RV7000 with the SpaceEcho preset mixed in at around 42 dry/wet. Finally, try adding a Scream 4 to the horns, using the Tape setting and dropping the Damage Control knob a little from its default setting. All these effects are routed automatically, as you can see in Figure 5.15. Finally, play in a simple horn riff. You can hear an example in the project file.

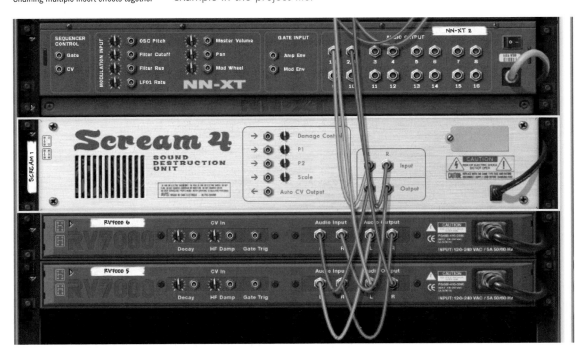

Another interesting thing to try is adding a Unison to the mixer as a send effect, then using the Aux send knobs for each channel to send varying amounts of signal through the effects. Try this and send the horns through it. You should find that it fattens up the sound quite a lot. If you raise the Detune knob on the Unison to around 100 and the Aux send on the horn's mixer channel to around 50 you will find that the trumpet sounds more life-like. This is just an example of how to add sends – you could just have easily added the Unison as an insert on the NN-XT that's playing the horns. However in a track like this, it is worth adding a little bit of Unison processing to various elements like the piano, guitars and even the tambourines. In this case it's more efficient to use one Unison as a send than many as inserts.

10 Break it down

Now try adding a bit of a breakdown. Copy a few groups of the tambourines and maybe the guitar, but leave everything else. Give MIDI focus to the bass by clicking the keyboard icon next to its sequencer track, and play in a different bassline for the duration of the break. Quantize it if you like, but not too hard so it retains its natural feel. It's good to throw in a few samples and effects over the top of the break too, like in step 5. Try adding a few more piano chords over the break too, but maybe only over the second part to give the track a bit of breathing space. If you like the new bass and piano lines you've created for the break, you could string them out to the end of the track rather than reverting to the originals. Simply copy and paste some more groups in, along with some instances of the original beats and samples.

File stage 9

Figure 5.16
How the arrangement might look

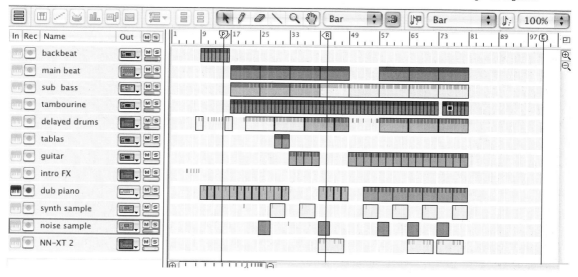

11 In the mix

Assuming that you're happy with the arrangement, it's time to move on to mixing. The first thing to do is add a Mastering Combi by selecting the Hardware Interface at the top of the rack and choosing Create > MClass Mastering Suite Combi. To be honest you can either get a mix then add the Combi, or add it then mix. Either way you will end up altering the mix to account for the changes the Combi creates to the sound, or tweaking the Combinator to account for the mix. The presets are a good starting point. The Hip Hop preset works well on this track. It tightens up the bass end without losing the middle.

File stage 10

Figure 5.17
Tweaking the Mastering Combi

Mixing is always subjective and will depend on your personal preference as well as the system you're monitoring on, but here are some ideas for this track. Try adding a compressor as a send to the mixer and sending a little of the drums and bass through it to emphasise them. It's important not to let the bass overpower the track, as the bass patch is pretty huge. The piano benefits from having a lot of the bass end rolled off on the mixer, and the treble emphasised a little. This makes it sit much better in the mix and sound less warm. Do the same with the horns, only this time roll off just a little of the bass. Find a setting that sounds good to your ears. It's also a good move to add a little reverb to the guitar using the main mixer's Aux sends, and make sure it sits just low enough in the mix. Remember that here it's a percussive instrument rather than a lead or melodic one.

The tablas should probably have some bass rolled off as the low parts of the loop interfere with the bass track. It's also useful to add a little compression and reverb to it. In the mix it should sit quite low, underpinning the main rhythm rather than competing with it. The individual hits you'll have to balance out as you go along, but it's easy enough as all the delay makes them blend very easily into the mix.

12 Fade to black

File stage 11

Once you're happy with the mix, try a fade out. You can just stop the track dead of course, or do a 'build down', but why not try a fade – it's very easy in Reason. Right click or control-click on the mixer and select Create > Sequencer Track for Mixer 1.

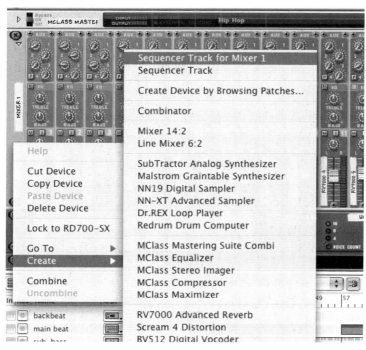

Figure 5.18
Automating a mixer fade-out

You can automate the mixer easily but like other modules it needs a sequencer track so that it can store the automation data, and you can edit it. You are probably familiar with how to automate by moving controls. Here, because the fade needs to be very smooth, why not draw it instead. Select the sequencer track for Mixer 1 that's just been created and enter Edit mode. Nothing is visible at first, so click on the button with the blue envelope on it to show the controller lane. Then from the menu next to that button, click and choose which controller lanes you want to view. In this case it's the Master Level.

Figure 5.19
Show Master Level Automation Lane

For reference you will need to set up a loop over the section you want to fade out, so you can see where to draw the ramp. To do this you may need to return briefly to the Arrange view to position the L and R markers. Another crucial step is to notice what level the master fader is at before you start automating. This is so that the master volume remains at that level right up to the point you want it to start dropping. Get it wrong and the level will judder up or down too quickly. In this case the level is 100, so using the pen tool, in Edit mode, click on the L marker at a value of 100. This value is then inserted for the duration of the project, meaning it won't unexpectedly change elsewhere. Then, simply use the line tool to draw a smooth ramp from 100 at the left marker to zero at or just beyond the right marker. This should give you a perfectly smooth fade out. After you have exported your track as an audio file you can use a wave editing program to 'top and tail' it to make sure there are no small clicks at the very start or end of the track.

Figure 5.20
A smooth master fade-out drawn with
the Line tool

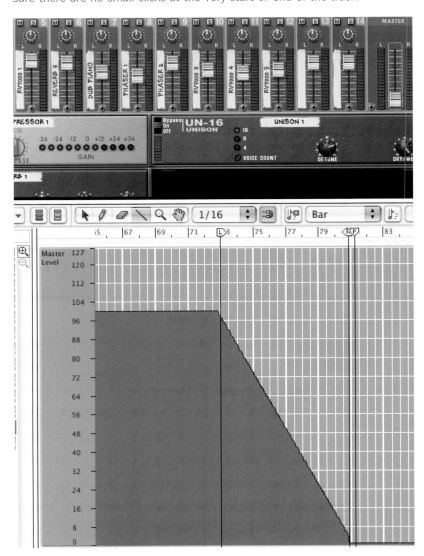

House

A brief history of house

House music originally grew out of Chicago in the late 1970s, where DJs like Frankie Knuckles at the WareHouse club used to mix disco records. In the early 1980s, drum machines became popular and started to give house music a more unique sound as DJs mixed disco records with new, harder beats. By 1985, house was becoming increasingly popular on the Chicago club scene, thanks partly to the growing availability of sequencers, better drum machines and synth basses like the still-popular Roland TB-303.

By the late 1980s, house had started to become popular in the UK, with early adopters like the Hacienda and Ministry of Sound helping it to take off. This would ultimately lead to the evolution of acid house and rave culture, and out of that would come Madchester, with bands like the Happy Mondays and Stone Roses borrowing elements of dance culture. Producers like Paul Oakenfold helped to bring the house sound to indie bands and create dance / rock crossover music.

Back in the States, despite tracks like Todd Terry's *Weekend*, and *Time for the Perculator* by Camjere being popular on the club scene, house was still not breaking into mainstream culture to any great extent. Although DJs like Armand Van Helden and Junior Vasquez were remixing many leading pop artist's tracks, it was a diluted form of pure house that some regarded as secondary.

At the end of the 1990s house had diverged into many different sub-genres including acid house, deep house, hip house, hard house, breakbeat, drum'n'bass and many others. The differences between them are sometimes obvious and in other cases they're more subtle. As the style from which all these have sprouted, house music is in many ways the father of modern dance music.

Recommended listening

Frankie Knuckles – *Beyond the Mix* (1991)
Paul Oakenfold – *Perfect Remixes* (2004)
Faithless – *Reverence* (1996)
Laurent Garnier – *30* (1997)
Coldcut – *People Hold On* (1989)
New Order – *Power, Corruption and Lies* (1983)
A Guy Called Gerald – *Automanikk* (1989)

The Workshop

1 Mechanical beats

House has always been music to dance to, emerging as it did from the club scene. As such, the beats are paramount, with four-to-the-floor bass drum kicks very much standard fare. A tempo of around 130BPM is a good place to start, and a lot of house doesn't stray too far either side of that kind of speed. House makes particularly extensive use of layered beats, so you may end up using the Dr.REX for some of the rhythms more than you would when writing in other styles. A beat is a good place to start with any kind of dance music, so create a REX player and navigate to the ReFills folder. There are a few good ones in there – try AMG Dance Diffusion > 189DANCE. This is a typical house beat. Use the To Track button on the Dr.REX to place the notes

Figure 6.1
Loading a dance REX loop

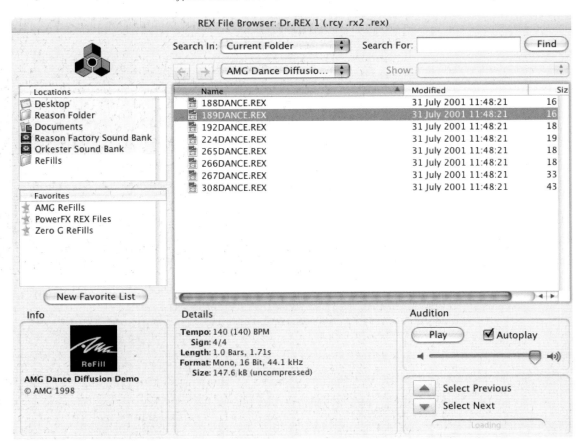

File stage 1

into the sequencer. Remember it will fill the space between the left and right markers. Try adding a compressor to the REX player and pushing the Ratio up to around 95. This immediately gives the drums a more punchy sound, especially the bass drum.

2 Organ grinder

Load up an NN-19 and find the patch from the Factory Sound Bank called Organ4.smp. Run a search if you can't find it, or look in the All Instrument Patches folder. You can use neutral organ sounds like this to help form the backing of a house track. You shouldn't use any heavy rotary effect on the sound, as it works best with just the smallest amount of modulation. Play in a riff. Three simple, syncopated chords will do for now, as you can hear in the example. The organ sound is really dry to start off with, so you need to do something to make it blend in more. One thing you can try is adding a Unison to fatten it up a bit – use a dry / wet setting of about 30, and a Reverb. Try

an RV7000 with preset 'The Met' set to about 20, just enough reverb so you can't hear the joins any more.

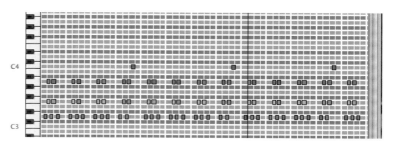

Figure 6.2
Building a melody line

Now try loading up a piano patch and playing a chord sequence that complements the first one. Try the NN-XT patch called 'A Grand Piano'. You should probably try to play something that harmonises with the organ riff but doesn't duplicate it. By doing that you'll start to build up the melodic element of the track.

The Piano could do with a bit of reverb, so try adding one as a send to the mixer and using the Piano's Aux 1 knob to apply some. You'll probably be adding a little reverb to most elements in this track so it makes sense to use send effects for at least some of it.

Now try adding some bass. Remember this is still really the build-up part of the track, so you don't want anything too heavy yet. There's a Combinator patch called House Bass in the Sound Bank which is perfect, so load it up.

Figure 6.3
Readymade Combinator patches sound great

It's actually a variation of the organ patch you've already loaded, just routed through some effects to make it much bigger at the bottom end.

Play a bassline that more or less follows the rhythm of the other two instruments that are playing. The bass usually syncopates, playing two long and then two short notes, which you can hear in the example file.

3 Build it up

File stage 2

If you're following the example file you'll see that things have built up gradually. The obvious thing to do is to build up to a short break and then come crashing in with the main beat. Before you do though, try stringing the intro out a bit longer. At higher BPMs, you get through the bars much more quickly. When the bass part comes in, try adding another rhythm. This time, use a ReDrum and load up some percussion. House Kit 8 from the Sound Bank has some good percussion sounds in it for this style. A simple, repeated pattern played over the other beat will do for now. Try using the hand clap, a great staple of house music. Use it on every second and fourth beat. Quantizing strictly to 1/16 is a good idea, as beats are fairly mechanical in house. Add a small amount of reverb to the ReDrum via the desk using its Aux 1 send knob.

Figure 6.4
Building up the arrangement

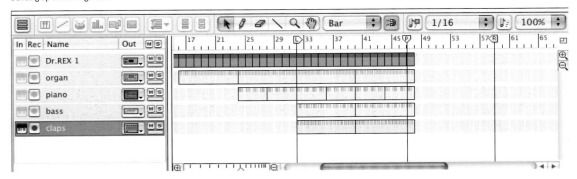

As you lead up to the next section of the track, here's an interesting and widely-used trick for signalling that something is about to happen. Wind the playhead back three bars before the end of the intro. Select the REX player that's currently playing the drumbeat, and automate its Filter Frequency control down, then up. The way to do this is to hit record and start moving the control down to zero over the first bar, hold it there over the second, and bring it back up to 100 or so over the third. You can see how this works in the example.

4 Step sequence the beats

File stage 3

The point of bringing the drums down and back up again like that is that when the track comes back in you can introduce the main beat, much heavier than the intro beat. Here's a good opportunity to have a go at programming a house beat. Load up a ReDrum and find a kit. House Kit 1 from the Sound Bank is pretty good. You can find a full description of how to step sequence drums in the chapter on techno, so if you're unfamiliar with the process, check it out first. Switch the Pattern Length button up to 32 – why not try programming a few variations later in the beat. Starting with the bass drum, switch the Dynamic button to Hard and program one bass beat on each of the eight first beats – so that's 1, 5, 9, 13, and the same pads for steps 17-32. Keep an eye on where the Edit Steps knob is, as the numbering of the pads won't visually change.

Channels 8 and 9 on the ReDrum contain two hi hats, so sequence them next. For the first four beats you could try putting a closed hat on beats 2, 6, 10 and 14, and then for the second four beats of the pattern, on 2, 5, 8 and 15. This is just an example of how it can work. It's probably better not to have exactly the same pattern all the way through the sequence – add a bit of variation. Experiment with moving beats around using the pads and see what works best.

Figure 6.5
Step sequencing with the ReDrum

Copy and paste the pattern to slot A2 on the ReDrum. Modify the pattern that's now in slot A2 to include a handclap. Here's a tip – program claps on pads 5 and 13 for both sections of the beat (steps 1-16 and 17-32). Now, press the Flam button at the bottom right corner of the ReDrum and click on pad 13 in both sections to activate flam. Set the Flam knob to about 22 so the double hit is really close together. This is a very subtle effect, but it differentiates the first hand clap from the second in each bar, even though it's the same sample.

Figure 6.6
Flam

Once you have some beats programmed into the ReDrum, (and you are free to create as many variations as you like), it's time to put them into the sequencer. You can automate pattern changes, as covered in other workshops, but you can also have Reason put the note data straight into the sequencer. Select pattern A1 and select the ReDrum's sequencer track. Choose Edit > Convert Pattern Track to Notes.

Figure 6.7
Convert Pattern Track to Notes

Then, choose the ReDrum itself and you'll see the Edit menu has changed. Choose Edit > Copy Pattern to Track, and the pattern is placed into the sequencer. Repeat with the pattern in slot A2 selected and any others you've created, and you can work with the beats as if you'd played them in by hand, as MIDI notes. Remember, once you have done this you must disable the ReDrum from playing its step sequencer, or you'll get weird phasing effects as the same beat plays doubled. Uncheck the Enable Pattern Section box on the ReDrum.

5 Dynamic effects for the beats

File stage 4

The next thing you'll want to do is beef up the sound of the main drums. Big beats is what it's all about. Set up a loop over the drum part you've just copied to the sequencer, and play it. Then choose Create > Combinator. Navigate to the Sound Bank > Combinator Patches > Effect Patches > Dynamics. As the drums play you can select different effects presets and hear how they suit the beat. The choice is yours, but Drums > Dirty Bass and Drum works well. Now, press Tab to spin the rack round. You'll see that initially, the ReDrum isn't routed through the Combinator, but that's easily fixed. Either drag the stereo outs of the ReDrum to the Combi Input ports on the back of the Combinator, or right-click / control+click on them and use the contextual menu to assign where they should go (Figure 6.8). The Combi is already routed to a mixer channel, so the signal path is now as it needs to be.

Copy the instrument data from the first part of the track in over the new beats. If anything, adding the effect Combi to the main beat has made it too loud and it overpowers the rest of the instruments! Drop its mixer channel a

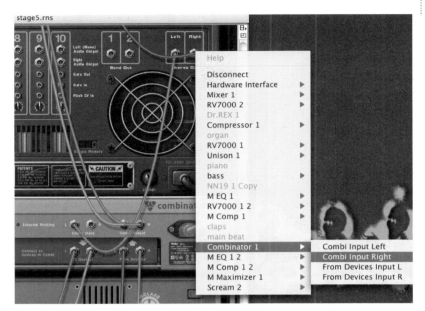

Figure 6.8
Contextual menu for assigning routing

bit to even the mix out, and try adding a small amount of reverb via Aux 1 send on the mixer channel for the ReDrum. Another thing you can try is clicking Show Devices on the Combi, locating the Scream 4 at the bottom and dropping the Damage Control knob a little. This has the effect of making the drums a bit less forceful. Play with the mixer channel and the Scream 4 settings until the main drums sound right. They should be powerful but not disproportionately loud.

Figure 6.9
The Scream 4 – warm up the sound

6 Adding more beats

At the moment there doesn't feel like there's enough of a gap between the intro and the point where the main drums come in, so duplicate the section with the main drums and then delete the first two groups. Also, delete the backing beat from the same section. You should now have four bars of just the instruments and the claps. Try adding a drum roll to lead up to the point where the main beat comes in. Create a ReDrum and load a good house snare sound into one of its channels. There's one in the Sound Bank called Sd3_SupaFunky that sounds good. The easiest way to program it is to go to Edit mode and draw in the notes using the pen tool. One bar's worth is usually enough. A bit of reverb added via the desk doesn't hurt, either.

File stage 5

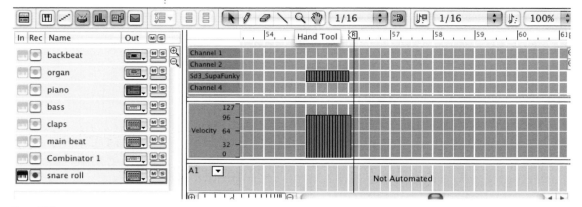

Figure 6.10
Programming a mechanical snare roll

Figure 6.11
Automating elements of the ReDrum

It's a good idea to fade the snare roll in, which you can either do by automating the mixer channel for the ReDrum (remembering to create a sequencer track for the mixer so it has somewhere to store the automation data) or by drawing it in the controller edit channel for the ReDrum. Enter Edit mode with the snare ReDrum selected and click the blue Show Controller Lane button, and then from the Controllers menu next to it, choose Drum Level for whichever channel you've put the snare in. In the example it's channel 3 (Figure 6.11).

The automation lane for the snare channel now appears, and you can draw a ramp from around 10 to around 100 over the duration of the snare beats. Here's a tip – you can start the ramp just before the beats, to ensure the automation doesn't miss a beat and cause jumping (Figure 6.12).

This is a good way to automate any aspect of any module. Remember that because a ReDrum has ten separate channels, each can be automated indi-

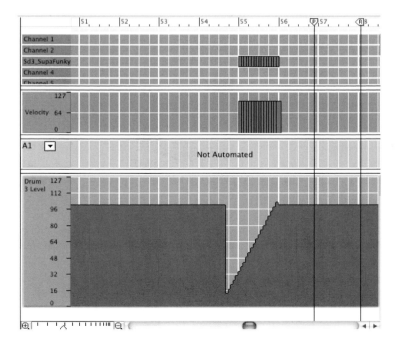

Figure 6.12
A smooth drum level knob automation ramp

vidually, giving you tremendous control over a kit even within a single drum sequencer. To finish off the roll, why not add a crash cymbal to play on the first beat of the next bar, to emphasise the start of the main part of the track. You can load one into the ReDrum you've just been automating. You can also copy and paste this fill at other points in the track to highlight breaks and transitions.

7 Damage control
After the main figure has played for a while, start to introduce some new elements. Load up a Combinator and have a look through the Sound Bank for some good Combi patches. There's one called Patternator which is great – it's incredibly complex if you look at how it's built, but you don't need to. The four knobs on the front panel are useful for tweaking the sound. If you turn the Pattern knob to around 65 and the Decay knob to about 40, you should get a sound that suits the track. Holding down a few simple notes does the trick. Try adding a Scream 4 to the Combinator as an insert effect. Then navigate to the Scream 4 patches folder in the Sound Bank and try the preset called Concrete Tunnel, which sounds pretty good. You may want to drop the Damage Control a little.

File stage 6

Figure 6.13
Scream 4 presets

Try putting a break in. A good trick is to drop most of the track out and leave just, say, the piano and the claps in. Maybe use a different riff this time for the piano, as in the example. Fast, repeated piano chords are a hallmark of house music. The House Piano preset on Korg's legendary M1 keyboard was the signature sound of a lot of early house music.

8 Adding punch to the drums

File stage 7

Try building on the break to take the track off in a new direction. Copy and paste the new piano riff for some extra bars, and load up another synth. This time, try using a Combi. Load up the patch called Juicer II from the Sound Bank. As you record some high notes from the Combi, play with the Mod wheel, which will provide a bit of variation to the sound. Now try copying and pasting a few instances of the break to extend it, and start to build it back up using the instruments that are already present in the track. Also, try adding a new backing beat instead of re-using the beat from the intro. To do this you might have to load up another Dr.REX and locate a good REX file. Try 125_HouseBeat_02 from the PowerFX folder. To add some punch to the drums, add a Combinator effect by selecting the Dr.REX with the new beat init and choosing Create Device by Browsing Patches. Then navigate to the Combinator effects > Dynamics > Drums folder and choose the Snare Bottom Mic preset – a really great drum sound.

Figure 6.14
Combinator effect patches

Name	Modified
At The Heart.cmb	2 Feb 2005 15:56
Big and Bright Drums.cmb	2 Feb 2005 15:56
Body&Punchy Snare.cmb	2 Feb 2005 15:56
Boomy SoftClip BD.cmb	2 Feb 2005 15:56
BoomyClick BD.cmb	2 Feb 2005 15:56
Bright Attack Snare.cmb	2 Feb 2005 15:56
Clicky BD.cmb	2 Feb 2005 15:56
Dirty Bass & Drum.cmb	2 Feb 2005 15:56
Drums.cmb	2 Feb 2005 15:56
FAT & LOUD Snare.cmb	2 Feb 2005 15:56
FAT Punchy BD.cmb	2 Feb 2005 15:56
Heavy Boomy BD.cmb	2 Feb 2005 15:56
Heavy Safe BD.cmb	2 Feb 2005 15:56
Hi Freq Snare.cmb	2 Feb 2005 15:56
Old School Snare.cmb	2 Feb 2005 15:56
RAW Boomy BD.cmb	2 Feb 2005 15:56
Snare Bottom Mic.cmb	2 Feb 2005 15:56
Tight Click BD1.cmb	2 Feb 2005 15:56
Tight Click BD2.cmb	2 Feb 2005 15:56
Top Mic Drums.cmb	2 Feb 2005 15:56

9 Shaking all over

File stage 8

After a few bars of this, copy a drum fill in and then copy the main drum part in too so that everything is playing. Why not also try adding a ReDrum, loading up a couple of shaker samples from the Sound Bank and adding a shaker part over this end section. You can play it in by hand but if you alternate so each sample plays every other eighth (meaning all 16 beats of each bar are taken up with shaker hits) you'll definitely need to quantize them to 1/16

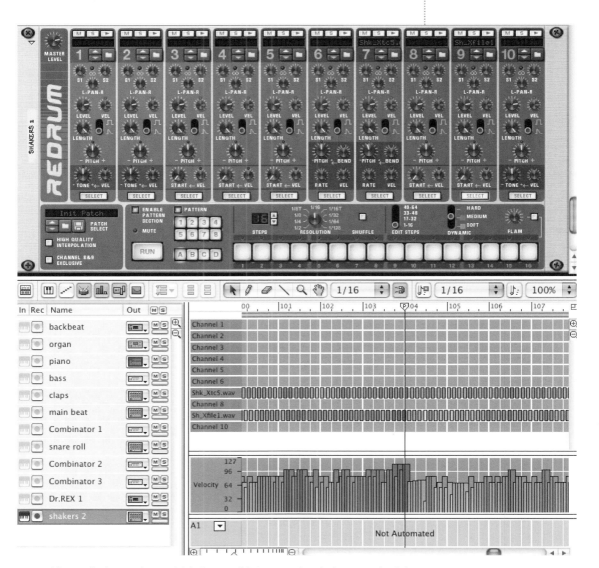

as at this resolution and speed it's impossible to get the timing exactly right by hand. The point of using two slightly different shaker samples is to achieve the effect of physically shaking a real instrument. Were you to use one it would sound too mechanical and lifeless. Leave the natural variations in velocity that occur when you play the keyboard in there – they add to the more natural feel.

Figure 6.15
Use two different samples to give the feeling of a real shaker

10 Starting to mix

Before you start mixing, add a Mastering Combi between the Mixer and the Hardware Interface. The Bass and Drum preset seems to be the most appropriate, although this will depend largely on what kind of sound you want and what you're monitoring on. If you do choose it, you might find that you need

File stage 9

to tweak the EQ within the Combi to bring back a little of the mid and hi parts of the track. The preset as it starts off boosts and compresses the bottom end nicely and makes it really punchy, but does limit the mid and top end a bit too much. You can of course compensate for this using the levels and EQ on the desk – mixing is a highly subjective process and it takes time to get it right. It's also worth raising the threshold on the compressor a little, so that when the bass comes in it doesn't pull the whole mix down too far. The main thing to make sure of when mixing is that the beats and the bass stay distinct from each other. The Mastering Combi does this to an extent, but use the mixer to balance them out too. Having a 'pumped' sound to the track is much more acceptable in house than in most other styles of music, where it's considered overkill. Make sure that the hi hats of the various drumbeats are clear enough to carry the track along, but not too hissy or tinny. Use EQs attached as inserts or on the mixer to smooth out any problems with the sound of individual instruments. The piano in particular may need its top end and level boosting to be heard over all the other sounds. With a little reverb applied to the drums and lead sounds, the whole track ought to sit together nicely. And then it's just a case of nudging faders until you're happy. Check out the finished example in file 10 for an idea of how it could turn out.

File stage 10

Figure 6.16
Mixing and Mastering

Techno

A brief history of techno

Techno in its earliest forms developed in the mid-1980s in and around Detroit, Michigan. Its pioneers are widely believed to be Juan Atkins, Derrick May and Kevin Saunderson. Emerging out of the house music scene, it initally had a lot in common with Chicago and New York house. As it grew in global popularity, producers based in Europe began to take it in different directions as it soundtracked the emerging rave and club scenes. Some notable artists have kept the original Detroit style going – people like Carl Craig and Richie Hawtin.

Techno is frequently entirely electronically generated, from the beats upwards. As such it has always been inextricably linked with sequencers and computers far more than real instruments. Often instrumental, the sequencer-driven nature of a lot of techno can inform the way it's composed – using sections of notes or beats to build tracks up or down. It's a way of working that is particularly familiar to Reason users. Melody and even groove are secondary to the beat and the rhythmic, mechanical tapping of the hi-hats and the 4/4 bass drums. Pure techno doesn't really rely on sampling to any great extent either. Conceived as a purely electronic style, the techno producer uses the sequencer or the computer and synths and drum machines as his orchestra. There's no limitation like you'd get with a band – in fact you don't necessarily have to be a skilled player. Programming skills are paramount. Pure techno is about syncopation and structure rather than any kind of traditional notion of songwriting. Classic synths and drum machines like Roland's 303 and 808 feature heavily, as do all kinds of other synths like Moogs, Oberheims, ARPs, Prophets and so on.

More recently a new kind of techno has emerged, embracing elements of rock, acid house, pop and even industrial music. It's hard to pigeonhole, but it started with The Prodigy bringing some sampling into their tracks as well as using sped-up, realistic-sounding drums rather than the synthesised drums associated with pure techno. Their album *The Fat of the Land* represented probably the most successful mainstream techno record ever made. Even more recently than that, bands like The Crystal Method have pioneered a sort of big beat / techno crossover, employing massive beats and acid synths, even introducing rapping and other vocals. Another great example of this is Overseer. Both have achieved considerable success by managing to make techno just mainstream enough to soundtrack countless video games and movies.

Recommended listening

Derrick May - *Rhythim Is Rhythim: Beyond The Dance* (1989)
Plastikman – *Sheet One* (1993)
The Prodigy – *Music For The Jilted Generation* (1995)
Underworld – *Dubnobasswithmyheadman* (1993)
Overseer – *Wreckage* (2003)
The Crystal Method – *Vegas* (1997)
Orbital – *Orbital* (1991)

The Workshop

1 Getting started

A good tempo to use for a techno track is somewhere between 130 and 140BPM. The project file is at 130, but if you like you can change it to make it slightly faster or slower. People start in different places when writing. Some start with a beat, others with a bassline or a hook. As techno tends to build up, with the main beats not coming in straight away, it would seem to make sense to start with a synth sequence. You'll also end up using the Matrix pretty heavily if you're writing techno, as it enables all kinds of great patterns that you couldn't play by hand. Before you start it's worth remembering that

Figure 7.1
Loading a rhythmic Malstrom patch

there are a lot of different variations on the techno theme – far too many to cover in detail here, but the walkthrough will give you good idea of how it all works. Start by creating a Mixer and then a Malstrom. Navigate to the Factory Sound Bank > Malstrom Patches > Rhythmic folder and load up a patch (Figure 7.1). T E E Chords works well.

It's not quite hard-sounding enough as it stands, so try switching the source of OSC B from Flute to 303 Loop. Play in a note and hold it. The patch is sync'ed to MIDI so it will perfectly follow the tempo of the track. Hold the note over four bars, as the sound evolves the longer you hold it for. Quantize the note so it falls precisely on the first beat of the first bar, if you think it's slightly out. Even though it's just one held note it's worth holding option / control + g to create a four-bar group, which will make copying and pasting far easier.

2 Scream and scream again

The Scream 4 is going to be one of your best friends during this workshop, and you'll soon see why. Attach one to the Malstrom as an insert (by selecting the synth then choosing Create > Scream 4) and select the Warp preset. Play back and you'll hear the sound immediately become much harder and sharper – much more authentic. In fact you may want to use the Cut section to roll off a little of the top end, as it can get hissy. Drop the damage control to around 40 – you don't want things to get too heavy yet. Copy and paste a few bars of this held note and set up a loop around it.

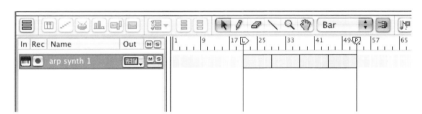

Figure 7.2
Grouping the notes

Now let's create a second synth hook to accompany the first. This time, create a Subtractor and try to find a good subtle patch for providing an Underworld – style sequence. The patch called Wheel Wah Lead from the Factory Sound bank is good. Remember at this stage you're still building up, creating a lead-in. It's worth lowering the Filter 1 Frequency control to around 22 to just back the sound off a little. If you want a really heavy sound you could try turning OSC 2 on. Let the first synth play for four bars and then play in a sequence on the Subtractor. Try something simple like a repeated three note pattern, as in the example. It's fairly important to quantize these strictly – use a setting of 1/16 and 100%. Group the new notes and then copy and paste them to fill the area you're working on. Try adding a compressor and a Unison to the Subtractor to beef its sound up a little bit.

3 Techno kits

Now try adding a beat, but start with something simple, just some hi hats. Load up a ReDrum and call up Techno Kit 1 from the Factory Sound Bank. There's a decent hi hat in channel 10 but it's worth changing the open hat

File stage 1

File stage 2

sound in channel 9 to something a bit better. Try the file called Oh_Xfile1. Here's an opportunity to use the ReDrum's onboard sequencer. On the ReDrum, press the Select button at the bottom of channel 10 so it lights up. Now the 16 pads become drum triggers for the hi hat sound. In this case you want the hats to play 16 beats at a resolution on 1/16, so you don't have to really change any timing settings. Click each of the pads so they're all lit. Initially it sounds a bit too mechanical, even for techno, because the velocity of every hit is the same. There's a simple way around this. If you alt + click on a pad it turns a lighter shade of yellow. This means its velocity is less, and so it's slightly quieter. By carefully mixing and matching full velocity with half velocity hits you can make the pattern sound interesting and not too uniform. In the example, pads 1,5,10,14, 15 and 16 are set to full velocity, and the rest to half. You can use the Dynamic switch to set pads to Hard as well if you like, but it's not necessary at this stage.

Figure 7.3
Specifying different dynamics for ReDrum hits on the step sequencer

Remember that you can audition ReDrum sequences independently of the song by using the Run button on its front panel. Each ReDrum has the ability to store four banks of eight patterns, so it's easy to store a whole series of evolving beats in a single one, and add them to the song later. Give it a try. Currently, the pattern you've recorded is stored in slot 1A. Select Edit > Copy Pattern and then click the Pattern 2 button and choose Edit > Paste Pattern. The pattern is now copied over. With this second pattern selected (2 and A should be lit) you can begin to add a little variation.

4 Flam, anyone?

File stage 3

Here's a great trick for programming drums. Use the Flam control at the bottom right corner of the ReDrum. With pattern 2 selected, click the small Edit Flam button, and then click on pad 15. The tiny red light above it will come on. You'll also hear a really cool fill has been added to the beat. You can raise or lower the Flam knob to make the fill even quicker or slightly slower, but the default value of 97 works well. Copy and paste this pattern into slot 3, as you pasted into slot 2 previously. Now add an open hat to the pattern. Click the Select button on channel 9 and experiment with adding a couple of open hats by triggering the pads. Switching on pads 7 and 15 adds just the right amount of variation.

Now that you have some beats for the intro, try adding them to the track. The way to do this is to select the ReDrum's sequencer track and enter Edit mode. What you want here is the Drum lane. Make a note of where you want to insert the patterns, and where your loop is. Switch snapping to Bar and move the playhead to the left marker. From the dropdown menu in the Drum lane, make sure it says A1 and then choose the pen tool. In the Drum lane, draw in four bars of pattern A1. Then for the next four, use the menu to change the pattern to A2 and draw in four bars of that. Finally, do the same

Figure 7.4
Using flam to create double hits

for the last four bars with pattern A3. These correspond to the three slots on the ReDrum into which you've saved patterns (Figure 6.5).

This process is fairly easy once you've grasped it. If you are struggling, check out Reason's manual, where it's described in great detail. Bear in mind that as soon as you start to automate drum pattern changes in this way, the ReDrum will insert patterns for the duration of the track. If there are parts where you don't want it to play, just set it to play an empty slot for those sections.

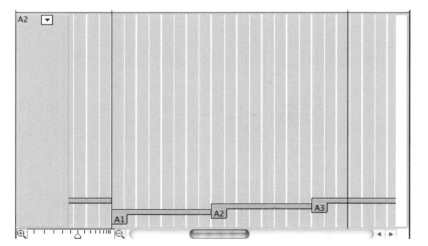

Figure 7.5
Automating ReDrum pattern changes in the Pattern Automation Lane

5 Acid leads

What you have so far is a good intro but still needs a little more building up. Create a Subtractor and load up a lead-style patch. Try Tech Lead 7 from the Factory Sound Bank. You can make it sound a bit harder by changing the waveform of OSC 1 to waveform zero and raising the Filter 1 Frequency slider to about 100. Also try activating the Low BW switch for some extra punch. Next, you might want to attach a Scream 4 to the Subtractor as well to dirty up the sound. Tweak the sound using the Scream 4, testing by playing your

File stage 4

keyboard. Try the Modulate setting, and drop the P2 Frequency control a little. You don't want too much distortion yet, so maybe also back off the main Damage Control knob to around 50. Try also adding a compressor and a delay to the Subtractor, with the delay dry/wet set to around 10 so as to just add a little depth to the sound.

You could try playing in a pattern by hand, or use the Matrix. Select the Subtractor and choose Create > Matrix Pattern Sequencer. This is great way to create some killer sequences. Don't worry about the signal path – the Matrix controls CV, not audio, so the Scream 4 will be routed separately.

Figure 7.6
Multi-chaining insert effects for a huge sound

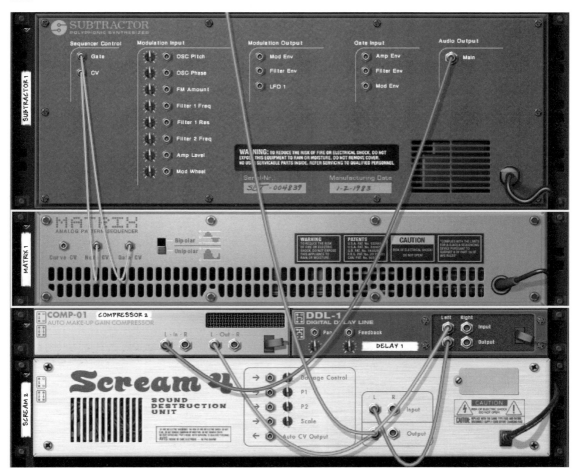

6 Matrix sequencing

File stage 5

Like the ReDrum's sequencer you can use the Matrix to audition patterns independently of the rest of the track using its Run button. The specifics of the Matrix are covered in detail in the manual, as well as in Propellerhead Reason Tips and Tricks, but here is how you can use it to quickly create some riffs. Use the octave control to move the Matrix's grid view down to 2. You can now draw data into the grid to make the Matrix play the synth. A resolution of 1/16 is good for this track, but you may not want every one of those

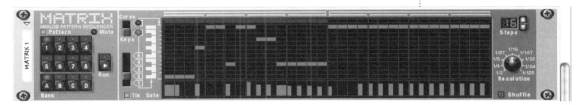

Figure 7.7
The Matrix is great at Techno patterns and arpeggios

16 notes to play. The bars along the bottom represent velocity, so if you drag them down to zero, no note will sound. If you want to hold a note, click the Tie button on the Matrix, and drag the gate bar between two notes. The note will then hold, as in the example. A good mixture of staccato and held notes usually makes for a realistic techno sequence.

If you play the track, the Matrix pattern will play the whole way through, so try rendering it down to the track. Select the Matrix's sequencer track and choose Edit > Convert Pattern Track to Notes. Then select the Matrix itself and choose Edit > Copy Pattern to Track. The same procedure for storing patterns applies to the Matrix as to the ReDrum, so you can copy and paste patterns between slots and create variations.

If you've copied the Matrix data to a sequencer track, you can use the Change Events command to randomize the pattern. Also if you're creating variations within the Matrix itself, try using Edit > Randomize / Alter pattern to have Reason do some of the hard work for you. If you use Alter Pattern, it keeps the original notes but alters their playback. Randomize changes every parameter. When you've finished copying data from the Matrix to the sequencer you don't have to delete the Matrix but you should probably disconnect its cables, as otherwise it'll play all the time. Be sure also to drag the notes you've transferred from the Matrix sequencer track to the Subtractor's sequencer track, so it will play correctly. You could also do this by reassigning the output of the Matrix's sequencer track to the Subtractor.

Adding electronic beats

Copy and paste so that the track occupies some more bars. Now try adding a main beat. An interesting trick is to leave four bars between the hi hats dropping out and the main beat coming in, as in the example. Create a Combinator, and from the Factory Sound Bank, load the Combi patch called Hybrid Electronic Drums. Run a search if you can't find it in the Combi patch folder. Play in a beat with a strict 4/4 bass drum and a mixture of closed and open hi hats. Quantize to 1/16 so it's tight. The great thing about this Combi is with all the ready-patched effects modules inside it, the beats sound good already.

The snare beats in this Combi aren't quite right for this track, so create a ReDrum and load up a snare sample to go over the top. Strangely, the kit called HeavyKit1 has an appropriate snare sound, although you'll need to tweak the level and pitch until it fits the track. Add a compressor and a Scream 4 with the Overdrive preset to the snare, and then record it over the existing beat. You can hear how this works in the example. You may also want to EQ the snare beat using the Cut section of the Scream 4.

File stage 6

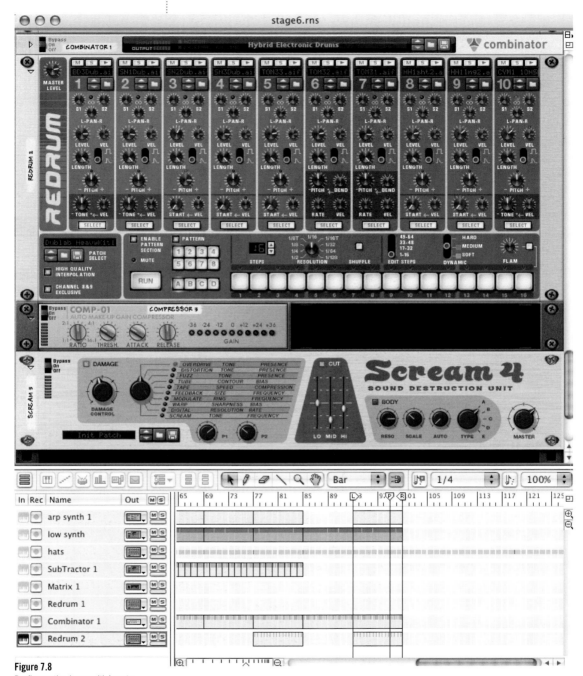

Figure 7.8
Beefing up the drums with inserts

File stage 7

8 Build up / down

A lot of the interest in techno comes from dropping elements in and out – that's also what makes it easier for DJs to mix tracks together. Try creating a 4 bar break by deleting some elements and just leaving drums and a synth, as in the example. Now create a Malstrom and try adding a pad sound over the break. Add a Unison and a compressor to make it sit better in the mix. There's still actually no specific bassline in the track, so create a Subtractor and add one. Try adding it after the break where you've just recorded the pad. Try the patch called Wonderbas. Keep the bass sound fairly simple – nothing too weird. Also bring the hi hats from the start back in at this point, as in the example. At this point it's a good idea to bring everything together for a full-on blast. In the example, the drums, bass and most of the synths are in. Try adding another sequenced lead synth. Leave the original one from step 5 out and try a new sound. Load a Malstrom and the patch TB302 from the Factory Sound Bank.

Figure 7.9
Phat Malstrom patches

9 Malstrom magic

This Malstrom sound is a fantastic bit of techno magic. It's very reminiscent of the kind of sounds that Overseer uses. You may want to turn the Shift knob on OSC B down to zero to stop the sound modulating quite so much, but that's a matter of taste. Attach a Matrix pattern sequencer to it like you did in step six. Create a pattern, or create several and save them into the different slots, just like you did with the ReDrum earlier. Remember to copy the notes you've placed into the Matrix's sequencer track onto the Malstrom's track and then disconnect the Matrix in the rack to stop it from playing per-

File stage 8

manently. Try running the Malstrom through a small amount of compression. You can fill out a lot of the rest of the track by creating new sequences to play with this Malstrom, and also with the Subtractor from the beginning of the track.

Figure 7.10
How it might look so far

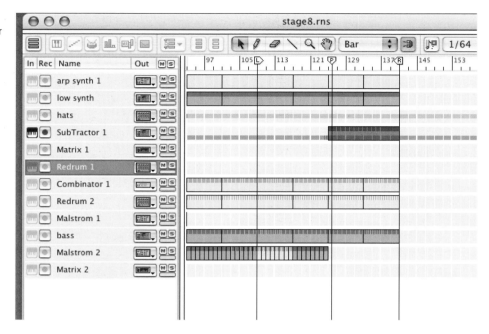

10 Punctuate the changes

File stage 9

To lead up to changes, you can use a snare roll and draw a velocity ramp. This is easiest to do in the key editor for a ReDrum. Set snapping to 1/16 and locate the bar before the change. Then use the Pen tool to draw in 16 snare beats, one in each grid slot. The use the Line tool to draw a velocity ramp so that they fade in right up to the end of the bar (Figure 7.11).

When you've done this, it helps the dynamic of the track to add a simple crash cymbal on the first beat of the next bar, just to really punctuate the change. As this ReDrum already has a kit loaded, use the crash on channel 10 and add in the note on the first beat of the next bar, as in the example. You will probably want to drop the pitch of the cymbal using its Pitch knob to make it sit better in the track. Use this snare roll / crash combo whenever you move between different parts of the track – it bridges them nicely.

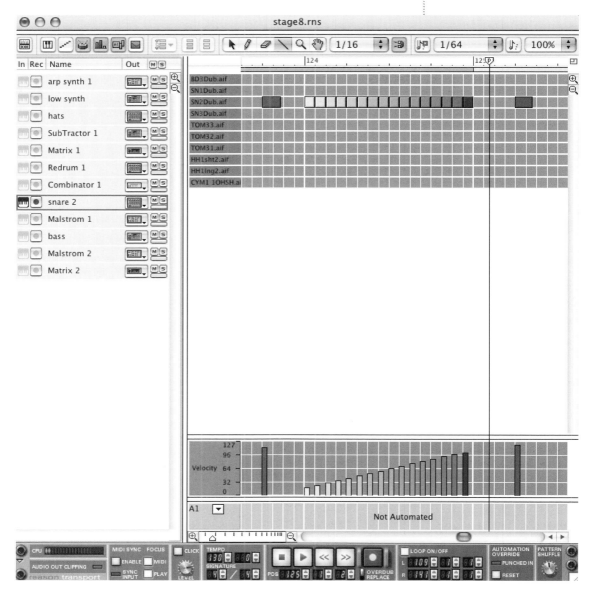

Arranging the rest of the track is a matter of taste (Figure 7.12). As mentioned before, it's about strategically bringing elements in and dropping them out. Luckily, it's made up of so many elements, synth parts and layered drums that this isn't all that hard to achieve. You might choose to do a build-down at the end, as in the example. It can sometimes work to end on a crash cymbal.

Figure 7.11
A snare roll

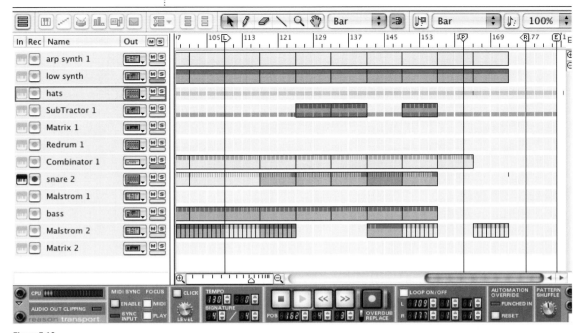

Figure 7.12
Arranging the track

File stage 10

11 Starting to mix

Before starting to mix, add a Mastering Combi between the Mixer and the Hardware Interface. Try the Dance preset. This introduces some fairly heavy limiting and compression to the whole mix, which in this case is along the lines of what you want to really pump the sound up. You'll need to maybe rein in the bottom end of the Subtractor that's playing in channel 2 as it's a bit bass heavy at the moment. Also since the introduction of the mastering Combi, the Subtractor in channel 4 is a bit too spiky and needs its top end rolling off.

The Combinator that's playing the bass drum needs its bass boosting a bit, as currently it's a little weak. You can either do this using the mixer's EQ knob or by attaching an EQ module to the Combinator. Either works well. Big bass drums are the bread and butter of techno and dance. The snare may need a bit of a hand too. Boost it using the ReDrum level control for its channel, number three. The Malstrom that's playing the really heavy lead line in channel 10 could do with a really small amount of reverb. Try adding one as a send connected to the mixer and using the Aux 1 control to add some to channel 10. A touch of reverb on some of the other channels won't hurt either.

The bassline, if anything, probably needs lowering just a touch, as there's quite a lot going on in the bottom end now that the Mastering Combi is doing its thing. Its heavy compression and limiting really affects the mix. You can tell if you bypass it – all the punch seems to drop out of the sound. One important thing to remember is that the hi hats should always be crisp and clear, carrying the track along.

File stage 11

Trip hop

A brief history of trip hop

Probably the youngest of the styles we're looking at, trip hop is a term originally invented not by the bands to whom it was applied, but by the music press. The bands themselves generally dislike the term and if pushed tend to prefer 'Bristol Sound', given that the style originated in Bristol, UK. Emerging from a combination of the hip hop and house scenes (although drawing much more heavily on the former), it's typically downtempo and atmospheric. Pioneers like Portishead and Massive Attack originally produced music that was quite sample-heavy, Combining rare breaks and loops with slowed-down hip Hop beats. Although they are frequently mentioned in the same breath, the two bands had substantially different approaches to composing. Massive Attack drew fairly heavily on dub and soul influences, while Portishead took a much more jazz and 1960s film soundtrack type of approach. If anything, Massive Attack's more famous tracks like Unfinished Sympathy have erred on the side of dance music, whilst Portishead's early work is a more textbook definition of pure trip hop.

The origins of trip hop's beats can be heard in the hip hop of of Eric B and Rakim, as well as snippets of Big Daddy Kane. That said, the production values are somewhat different, favouring real instruments, minimal guitars, Rhodes, Hammonds and even strings. Traditionally, trip hop has been exquisitely produced, but pains have been taken to make it sound lo-fi as well. This can involve various recording techniques like sampling your own recordings, or leaving in the hiss and crackle from vinyl samples. Composing trip hop generally involves some musical dexterity, as melodies and themes tend to be more musically complex than, say Hip Hop, where it's more about the beats and scratches.

Trip hop in its original form hit the peak of its popularity in the mid-1990s. Since then like many other styles it's been subverted and diluted, taken off in different directions all of which bear a relation to the original Bristol Sound but don't replicate it. Bands like Morcheeba have taken it in a more pop direction, Zero 7 and Air have perfected more ambient, electronic forms of trip hop and there's a fair amount of instrumental stuff out there too. In fact it's debatable whether pure trip hop exists any more, with originators like Massive Attack and Tricky releasing albums that bear little relation to their early works.

Recommended listening

Portishead – *Dummy* (1994)
Massive Attack – *Blue Lines* (1991)
Sneaker Pimps – *Becoming X* (1996)
Tricky – *Maxinquaye* (1995)
Zero 7 – *Simple Things* (2001)
Crustation – *Bloom* (1998)

The Workshop

1 Getting started

Trip hop is characteristically laid back, so a tempo of between 65 and 85 BPM should do. The project file is at 70, a happy medium. A good place to start is with a Rhodes riff or chord sequence, so call up an NN-XT and load up the TremRhodes patch from the Factory Sound Bank, or something similar in an NN-19 – say the RhodesMKII patch. It's got a bit of a tinny sound to it, which is often the case with sampled Rhodes. You can get rid of it though. The bell sound comes right at the start of the sample, so by raising the Sample Start knob to around 35 you can cut it off and leave a really warm, round sound. The sound is dry and as such pretty lifeless, so try adding a reverb unit as an insert. An RV7000 with the FilmScore preset and dry/wet set to 10 seems to work well. Activate the click and play in a chord sequence that will form the starting point of the track. Something simple and uncluttered, like in the project file. Don't quantize it too strictly – leave some of the natural feel in there.

Figure 8.1
A mellow Rhodes with a sweet reverb

Now try introducing a beat. Nothing fancy to start with, maybe just a very simple, fairly dry rhythm with just hi hats, bass and a rimshot. Create a ReDrum. The best option here is to load a few separate drum samples into the drum channels rather than trying to find a whole kit. If you click on the name fields in each of the channels, they will give you a quick list of available types of drum for that channel, which saves time. Here's a tip – the bass drum sample called Bd1 Boom is excellent here. Use the Browser to search for it if it doesn't appear in the list. It's deep enough but too boomy, so use the Length control on its ReDrum channel to tighten it up. A setting of 45 works well. In the example, Rim2_Dentaku and Hh3_Monk are the other samples used. Now you have a very basic but atmospheric kit. Try playing in a simple beat over the Rhodes chords. It may help to activate the click for this part. Quantize the drum, but not too tightly. In the example, a value of 1/16T and 75% has been used. It's worth running the ReDrum through a little compression and reverb, and you'll also want to balance out the different drum sounds using the level controls on the unit itself. Use a relatively low threshold on the compressor to control the bass drum.

Figure 8.2
A minimal drum kit composed of separate hits

2 Big bass

Now try adding a bassline. Synth basses aren't used that much in trip hop, so try calling up an NN-XT and loading a big, fat electric or an upright bass. The sound shouldn't have any slap or chorus about it at all, as that will kill the atmospherics of the music. In the example, the patch Upright+Harm is used. Bring it in after 8 bars of the drum part have played, or whenever it feels to you like the bass should come in. After a few bars of this you might want to break into the main part of the track. Try adding a new drum part in a ReDrum. Abstract Kit 1 from the Factory Sound Bank works well (Figure 8.3).

It's worth replacing one of the hi hats with a ride cymbal. Do this by clicking on the name field and choosing a new sample. Rd1_Rare works well, and will replace the hi hat beat in carrying the track along. You'll get a better sound by lowering the pitch of the bass drum slightly and maybe also replac-

File stage 1

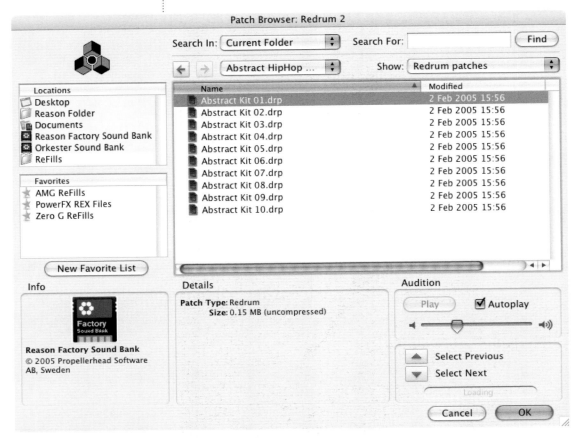

Figure 8.3
The main kit

ing the snare sound with a better one. The sample Sd_Abstract is good, especially if you add a reverb as an insert and route some of the snare through it by patching the snare channel through the reverb from its ReDrum channel. Play in a beat. A regular beat with 8 ride hits and the bass and snare hitting alternate beats sounds good. Figure 8.4 shows the routing. Balance out the elements of the kit using the pitch, length and level knobs on the ReDrum. Also try adding a compressor to the drum kit with a Ratio setting of around 40 to even out the dynamics.

A little scratching

File stage 2

As part of the drum patch there's a scratch sample, which sounds good if thrown in occasionally. However it's rather dry as it stands, and would benefit from some delay. Create a delay unit and hold down shift as you do so. This creates an unpatched module. The press tab to spin the rack around and route channel 7 of the ReDrum into the delay unit, and the delay out to a new mixer channel. Try using a delay setting of feedback set to 70 and dry/wet set to 50, as in the example. So you should now have a few bars of rhodes, bass and drums. Try creating a break. Load up a Dr.REX player and find the file AMG ReFills > King Tone Grooves > 5702_KTG. At first it has the wrong sort of sound for this track, so try adding an ECF filter and

Figure 8.4
Around the back

Figure 8.5
Create a sequencer track so you can
automate the filter

automating a filter sweep. This is more of a dance
music technique, but it can make for an interesting
effect in other styles too. Set up a loop and use the
Dr.REX's To Track button to place some data onto
the sequencer track. Create a sequencer track for the
filter module by right-clicking or control-clicking on it,
as shown in figure 5. Now play back the loop and hit
record. Use the controls on the ECF – mostly the frequency control – to morph the filter over time.

Enter Edit mode with the Filter's sequencer track
selected and you can view the automation you've just
created. If you like you can smooth it out using the
pen tool. Now create a sampler and find some good
one-shot sounds to play in over the break. Zero G
ReFills > Ambient Textures > NN19 > Ending 1 is a
good bet. Try running it through some delay.

Figure 8.6
Create a break

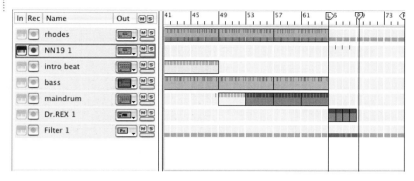

4 Making arrangements

After the break is a good time to bring everything back even stronger than before. In a moment this will involve using some strings. First, copy in some groups of the Rhodes, bass and main drums after the break. To emphasise the start of the new section of the song, a good trick is to use a crash cymbal to punctuate the first beat of the bar. Load a ReDrum and into one of its channels, load the relevant sample. The best place to look is in the Factory Sound Bank > ReDrum Kits > xclusive drums folder. Find a crash cymbal and route it through a little reverb, either as an insert or as a send via the desk. Quantize it to fall exactly on the first beat of the bar when everything kicks in. The crash should be fairly low in the mix – too high and it sounds really unnatural. If in doubt, keep it lower rather than higher. The reverb helps it to blend into the mix anyway. In fact you could copy the crash hit to the first beat of all the main sections, or whenever anything significant is built up to. Don't use it too much though or it gets wearing. On top of the Rhodes chords, it might be nice to add a melody. If you were recording audio in another program with Reason ReWired to it, you might want to put some guitars or sax on. Too keep it in-house and still sounding good, why not try a Piano? Load an NN-XT and find the Grand Piano patch from its folder on the Sound Bank.

What you play here is up to you but something jazzy always sounds good in trip hop. Check out the example in the project file to see how you might want to proceed with the piano part. It has been quantized, but only a little, to retain its slightly lazy, behind-the-beat sort of feel.

File stage 3

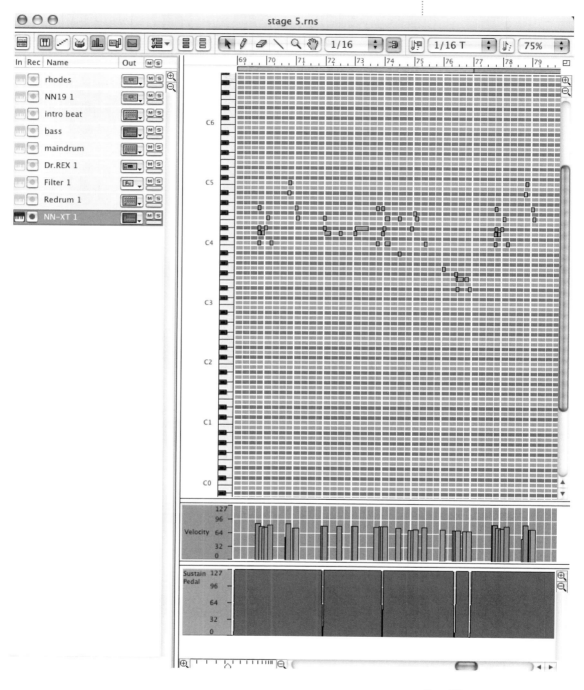

Figure 8.7
Playing jazzy piano chords

5 Break it down

Bt the end of the file 'stage 4' you should have the beginnings of the main theme of the track. After a few bars of the piano, why not have a tiny break and then bring in some strings? To signify that a change is about to happen, it's often good to drop almost everything out for just a beat or two, to provide some breathing space and to tell the listener that something bigger is invariably about to appear. In Figure 8.8 you can see that the same section has been repeated, but for the last two beats of the middle bar, the bass and most of the drums have been removed. To delete specific bits of a group you'll need to either turn snapping off, or set the snap value to something like 1/16 so you can drag the boundaries of a group around more freely and edit notes without having to go into Edit view. To delete elements of a drum part from a single sequencer track you'll definitely have to go into Edit view.

Figure 8.8
Arranging the track

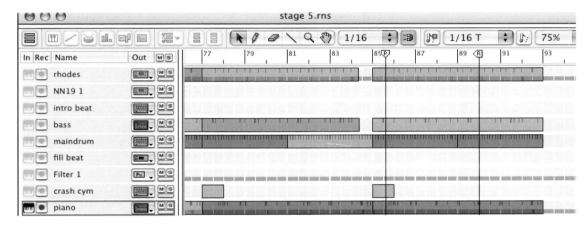

6 Stringing it along

Now you get to play with Reason's rather excellent Orkester Sound Bank. The NN-XT is the instrument best suited to using the multi-layered patches it contains, so create one. Go to the Strings section of Orkester and try some patches. You want something warm but subtle. The patch called VNS+VCS+BSS is a safe bet. The strings sounds needs a bit of managing to make it blend into the mix. Your first step could be to add some reverb as an insert. It's well worth soloing up the strings when you do this so you can see how the effects are changing the sound independently of the rest of the track. Try a compressor too, with a relatively low threshold of around -28 to keep the strings from becoming overpowering.

7 Guitar wizardry

With a little arranging, you can build the track up so it becomes quite full. How you do this is a matter of personal preference, but in the example file 6, it builds up to an almost orchestral arrangement with the strings. There are a few flourishes in terms of accompaniment that you might want to try. Here's one. Select Create > Create Device by Browsing Patches and search for an NN-XT patch called Gt TremoloChords. This is a rather nifty readymade guitar chord patch that sounds really good.

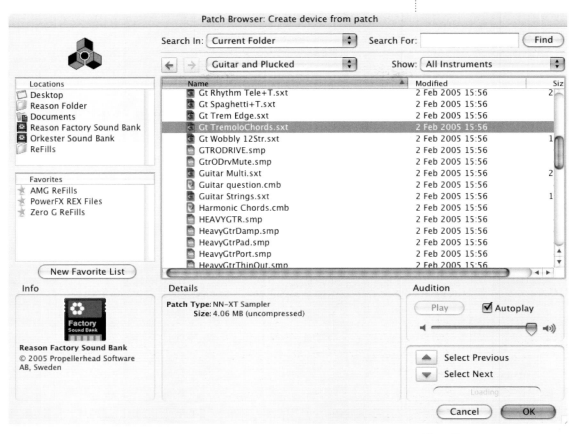

Figure 8.9
Locating guitar samples from the Sound Bank

As the chords are played by a single key, you may not have enough chords to exactly fit what you've written for the rest of the track, but the chances are you'll have some that fit. In the example, playing C and F triggers two chords that fit with the track. Keep the guitar relatively low in the mix and apply some reverb to it. It's more of a percussive than a lead instrument in this context.

8 Build-down

As the track comes to an end you could try fading it out by performing an automated fade on the master fader, but why not try doing a build-down instead? Start by dropping out the Rhodes, then later the main drums and the strings. You could also try bringing back the drums from the intro to help the track play out to the end (Figure 8.10).

If you do this, try ending on a single guitar chord, as in the example. Hold the note a little longer so it tails off properly. Before you start to think about mixing the track, add a mastering Combi between the Hardware Interface and the mixer. This will change the sound dramatically so it's worth doing before you start to mix the track.

File stage 7

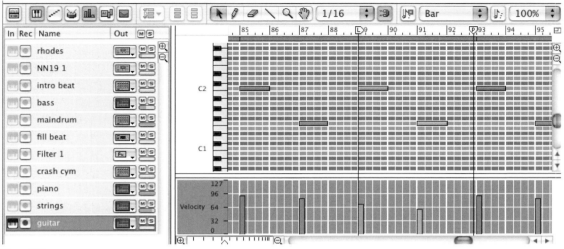

Figure 8.10
Triggering the guitar sample

File stage 8

Figure 8.11
Getting the mix right

9 Mastering your sound

The Kompakt Mastering preset on the mastering Combi works well as a starting point for this type of music. When mixing, Rhodes sounds tend to be quite warm and large, so you might need to roll off a little of the top and bottom ends using the mixer EQ to rein it in a little. Make sure the bass and bass parts of the drums aren't too boomy. This might mean adding compressors to the bass sampler and maybe even re-routing bass drum channels out of ReDrums through compressors and then out to the main mixer.

The main drum part should be spacious but tight – EQ the ride cymbal so that it carries the top end of the track along. For a good example of how this works, listen to anything by Portishead or Zero 7. The piano should tinkle lightly over the top of the track, but use enough reverb to make it blend in properly. The guitar should sit relatively low in the mix, but probably should-n't have any weird effects on it, as this doesn't fit with the style. A little compression and reverb are all that's really required.

10 Restrain the strings

The strings are important to get right as they can take over if not properly mixed. Hopefully by this stage you have them running through a compressor and a reverb already, so any further tweaking of the sound can probably be done using the mixer's EQ, or by attaching a PEQ-2 to the sampler that's playing the strings. If you're EQ'ing the strings or anything else it makes sense to do it while the rest of the track is playing. This is because you're trying to make a sound fit into the track. On its own it may sound too thin, but in the context of the track it could be perfect. EQ'ing often involves taking some of the bottom end out of bigger sounds to stop tracks from becoming too bassy.

11 Warm up the sound

As a final touch, you could try adding a Scream 4 between the mastering Combi and the Hardware Interface (Figure 8.12). This will ensure the whole signal is passed through it. For subtlety, try choosing the Tape preset and dropping the damage control down really low. This should give you a lo-fi tape effect over the whole track. However you may find that this doesn't work well for you – it will depend on the track you've made and your own ears. If it doesn't, just remove the Scream 4. You may well find that the mastering Combi has given the track enough punch already.

File stage 9

Figure 8.12
Passing the entire mix through a tape saturation simulator to warm it up

Trance

A brief history of trance

Many believe that trance is a sort of fusion of techno and house music, because initially it had a similar tempo and beat to Techno, but also the slightly more melodic and musical elements of House. It was intended to be hypnotic, putting the listener into a trance-like state, hence the name. As such, it originally consisted (and still does in some circles) of fairly long build-ups and build-downs of repetitive beats and patterns.

It originated in Germany at the turn of the 1990s. By the mid-90s, it was hugely popular on the club circuit, with producers like Armin van Buren and Paul van Dyk playing up the epic, anthemic side of trance, with massive lead synths and pads replacing the subtler elements that had previously been its hallmark. Paul Oakenfold, one of the best-known trance DJs and producers, was pioneering the music in clubs and helping it to become one of the most commercially successful genres. By the end of the 1990s, trance had split into a large number of sub-genres, including Goa, Progressive, Hardcore, Hard, Anthem and Acid. Early adopters like Sasha and Digweed went on to produce trance that was darker, sometimes known as 'deep' trance.

Entirely synthesized, with some sampled vocals and avoiding real instruments almost without exception, trance is inextricably tied to sequencers, drum machines and synths. Heavy use is made of compression, reverb and delays, especially on lead lines, to lend it a huge, club-filling sort of sound. Arpeggiated patterns also feature extensively. Trance is also unusual in that it's probably the most mechanical of any of the styles we've looked at. Musically it's fairly minimal, relying on some simple riffs and a few large lead-line hooks. It also tends to use fairly simple chord progressions, and break-downs rather than variations to maintain interest. Reason's modular nature and the fact that you can keep layering synths and effects on top of each other makes it a perfect tool for producing trance music.

Recommended listening

Paul Van Dyk – *45RPM* (1994)
Jam and Spoon – *Tripomatic Fairytales 2001* (1993)
Hallucinogen – *Twisted* (1999)
Paul Oakenfold – *Tranceport* (1998)
Chicane – *Behind the Sun* (2000)
BT – *ESCM* (1997)
Eat Static – *Abduction* (1995)

The Workshop

1 Getting started

Trance is fairly fast-paced, so a tempo of between 130 and 140BPM is a good starting place. It's also all about the build-up, although you can start with a beat or with a riff, depending on how you want to proceed. Try starting with a riff. You'll make heavy use of the synths and filter automation here, so it's worth knowing a bit about them before you start. Create a Subtractor. Why not try making your own patch by modifying the default settings? First, switch on OSC 2, and then detune OSC 1 by 12 and OSC 2 by -12. This has the effect of fattening up the sound. Raise the Mod wheel on the Subtractor to just above halfway, and raise the Filter Envelope Decay to around 45.

The sound is still far too dry, so you'll need to add some fairly hefty effects as inserts to bring it up to speed. First, add a reverb. A good one to try is a Combinator with the Compressed Reverb setting. Open the Combi and try

Figure 9.1
Getting started with a Subtractor

raising the dry/wet of the RV7000 a little higher – say to around 35. You use more reverb in trance music than in any other styles we've looked at. Next, try adding a Scream 4 to add some weight to the sound. Not too much crunch though – try the Distortion setting, with the Damage control at around 50. You could also use the Cut section to boost the frequencies slightly. Finally, add a delay unit. A simple DDL-1 will do , with dry/wet set to around 45, as in the example. Now try playing a melody in. Try something simple – just a few repeated, syncopated notes that go up no more than about five notes or so. Over the top, play the same pattern, only harmonised one octave plus a third above. Check out the example file to see how this works – it's a textbook trance melody. Quantize is strictly to 1/16.

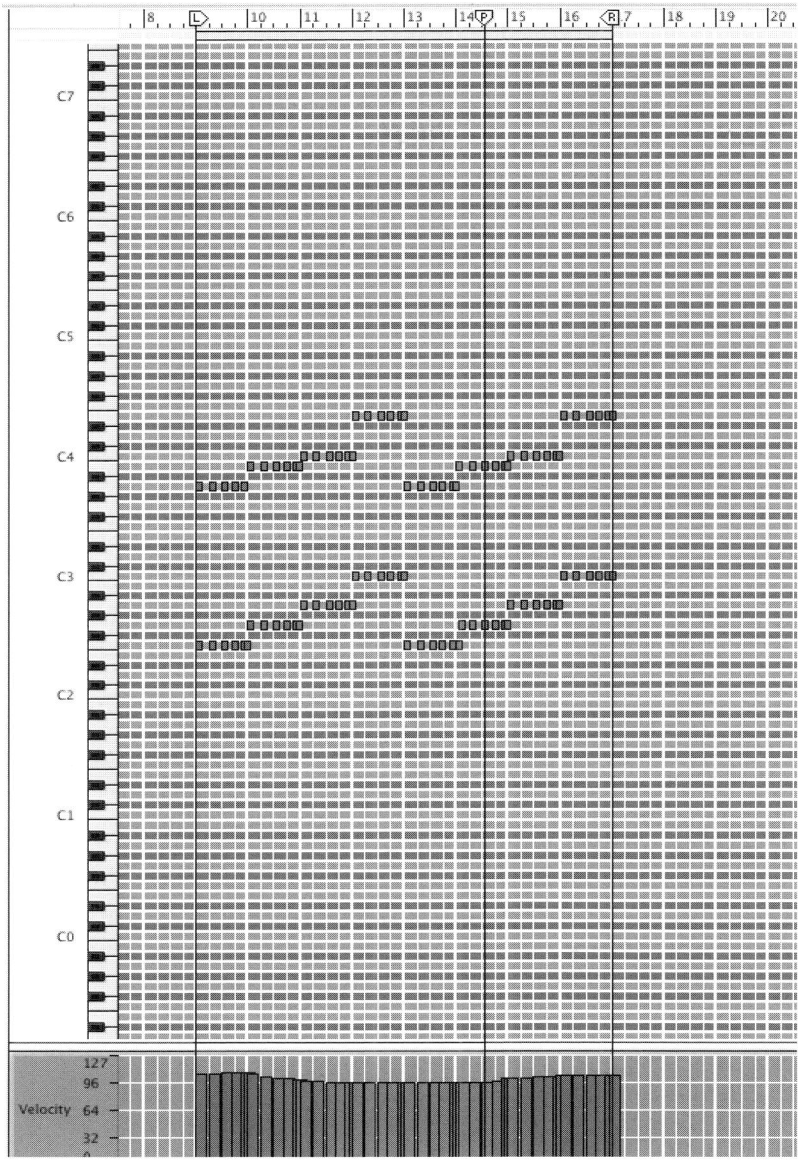

Figure 9.2
Playing in a simple repeated pattern

Automatic for the people

Here's the first of many filter automations that you're going to do. Locate the Filter 1 Frequency slider on the Subtractor and drag the playhead back to the start of the track. Duplicate a few groups of notes so you've got something to work with. As you play back, drag the Filter 1 Freq slider slowly up from zero to around 90. If you like you can double click on the MIDI notes in the sequencer, to view or edit this automation data in Edit view. If you do this, it's easier to achieve a smooth ramp by using the Line tool to draw one in. Try automating a filter sweep over about 16 bars. You'll see the filter gets a green box around it, and now moves by itself, replicating the movements you

File stage 1

Figure 9.3
Automating parameters

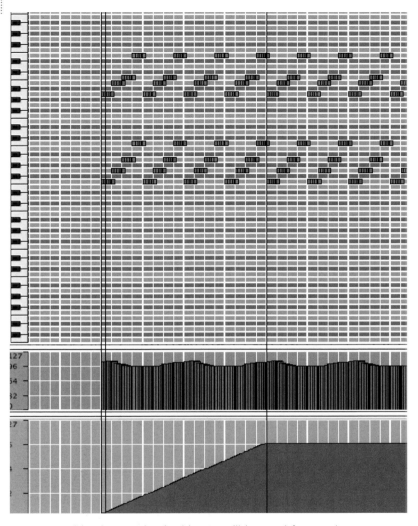

programmed in. Automating in this way will be used frequently, so remember how it's done (Figure 9.3).

Here's a good trick for trance. You need really huge synth sounds, and the easiest way to get them is by having several synths play the same melody. In Reason this is simple, as all you have to do is copy sequencer data between tracks. Even automation data is copied to save you time. To this end, create a Malstrom and load a patch – try the one called Velodront.xwv from the Sound Bank. It will sound better if you deactivate OSC A entirely, leaving just OSC B on. Use Copy and Paste or alt + drag to duplicate the sequencer data from the first track to the second 16 bars of track 2. Try adding a reverb to the Malstrom. Remember, its purpose is to back up the original synth, not fight with it. It doesn't matter if the Malstrom sounds a bit thin on its own, it only matters that it sounds good when it's playing along with everything else.

Create some beats

Now try adding an intro rhythm. Load up a Dr.REX and go to the PowerFX ReFills folder, where you'll find a REX loop called 140 Trance 11 Hihat. Use the To Track button to transfer the beat to the sequencer where the second synth comes in. Duplicate these groups of notes a few times so that the track extends a bit further. Now think about adding a bassline. Create a Subtractor and load up a large bass patch – something fat but without too much attack or squelch. This isn't techno, remember. There's one called MKS Fivedee that sounds good. Play in a bassline that fits with the track. Something simple will do – alternating notes, one octave apart. Quantizing to 1/16 is pretty important too, as it'll help keep the track tight.

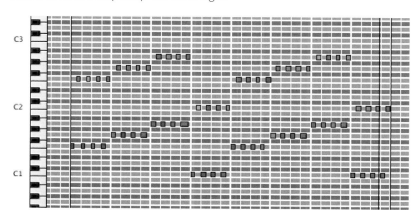

Figure 9.4
Trance basslines

The bass needs a little boosting, so why not try attaching an effect Combi to it as an insert? The preset Dynamics > Bass > Deep Bass sounds good on this particular patch.

After all this has run for 16 bars or so, try pasting the filtered synth from the start of the track into place after the other instruments stop playing. This is a common trick – to drop practically everything out and come back in with a massive beat shortly afterwards. You could also try pasting eight bars' worth of the bassline in, but automating its Filter 1 Frequency slider so it fades out before everything comes back in. You can hear and see how this works in the example file.

4 Gathering storm

Let's try really building things up even more before bringing the main drumbeat in. Add another Malstrom and load a big synth string patch. Something like String Machine from the Sound Bank will do, and run it through some reverb. This will really build up the tension effectively before the track comes crashing back in. Duplicate a few more bars of the break – as many as you feel is right – and play some simple chords using the string patch that follow the chord sequence of the rest of the track. To lead into the next section, use a repeated snare roll that fades up to the point where the main drums are going to kick in. Load up a ReDrum and load a snare sample into one of its channels. There's one in the Sound Bank called Sd2 Hardknox that sounds good. Use the Browser's search function if you can't see it at first. The easiest way to achieve a roll is simply to go into Edit mode and draw the notes into the ReDrum's Drum lane.

Over four bars, create the drum roll. The easiest way to do it is to draw a single beat at the very start of the loop, then set snap to 1/16 and just use copy and paste to create the rest. Reason will automatically paste a note exactly every 1/16 of a beat, which is far easier than trying to play or draw them in by hand. Then, to simulate the drum roll fading in (as is common in most forms of dance music), automate the Level knob for the ReDrum channel into which you have loaded the snare hit, in the same way you automated the filter on the Subtractor earlier. You could of course automate the Master Level knob for the ReDrum, although if you went back later to add any further sounds to this ReDrum, they would be affected too, so it's easier at this stage to just automate the individual channel's level.

Figure 9.5
Automating a snare roll so it fades in

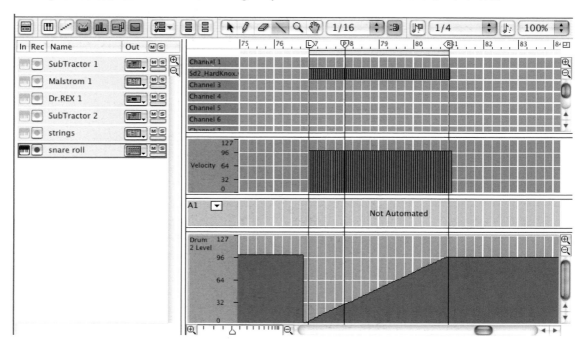

5 Big beats

File stage 4

Now for the main beat. You may have some great trance beats as REX loops, in which case you can of course use one here. Alternatively, try programming your own. Create a ReDrum and load a kit up. Try House Kit 8 from the Sound Bank. The beats are fairly relentless and don't really vary all that much so it might be a good idea to program the ReDrum using its built-in step sequencer. You can find more detail on how to operate the sequencer in the Techno chapter, step 3. The bass drum should play every beat, and the hi hat immediately after every bass hit. Use a clap instead of a snare drum, as snares often feature in trance only for the purpose of fills and rolls.

At the moment the beat probably sounds pretty lifeless, but you can spice it up a lot by adding some effects. As there are some great ready-made effect

Combis, why not take advantage of them. With the ReDrum selected and playing, choose Create > Create Device by Browsing Patches. This will let you audition the effects from the Browser without having to commit to using them. There's a patch in Dynamics > Drums called Dirty Bass and Drums that sounds brilliant. It takes care of the punch, but you'll still need some reverb. Repeat the process (with the ReDrum selected) and this time choose a reverb patch, like Reverbs > Compressed Reverb. You might want to open up the Combi and use the dry / wet knob to drop the reverb a little, say, to around 10. With the ReDrum's sequencer track selected, choose Edit > Convert Pattern Track to Notes. Then choose the ReDrum in the rack and choose Edit > Copy Pattern to Track. This will place the drum part into the sequencer. Remember to uncheck Enable Pattern Section on the ReDrum, or it will duplicate the drum part, which you don't want.

Figure 9.6
Programming the ReDrum

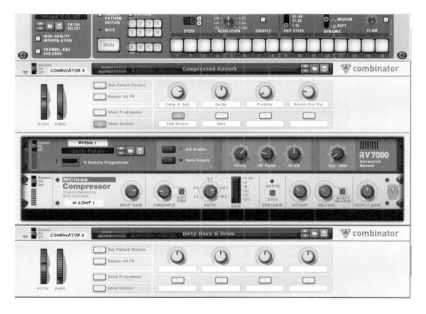

Figure 9.7
Heavy effects processing for a huge sound

File stage 5

6 Piano magic

Now that you've got a bit more content you can start to do some arranging. After the drum roll, copy and paste in the rest of the parts you've created so far, including the bass, the hi hats and of course the drum part you just made. The next step is to add some variation in the lead lines. One thing to try is to introduce something like a piano, but a piano in a House style. Create an NN-19 and load up something like the GrandPiano Thin patch from the Sound Bank. Raise its Filter Frequency slider to around 60, which will give the sound a much more 'dance piano' feel. Also, add a DDL-1 delay as an insert, which will cause the piano to blend in much better with the rest of the track. Try playing a simple, monophonic melody line, fairly high up on the keyboard. It's a common technique in trance and House music. Check out the example file to see what it can sound like. Also try using a compressor on the piano with the Ratio set to around 100, which will help it to stand out of the mix a bit, especially when competing with everything else. Try starting the riff right

Figure 9.8
A special fx piano sound

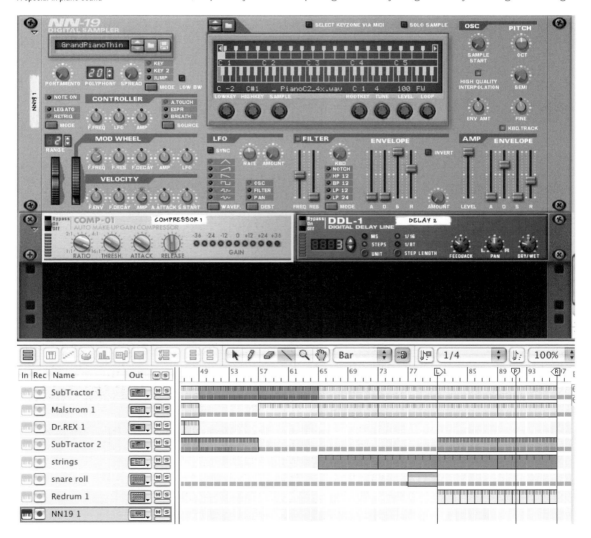

before the main beat comes in – you hear this trick used a lot in trance. You may also find you have to bring the drums out a little, in which case you could try adding a Unison as an insert to the ReDrum to fatten up the sound (Figure 9.8).

7 Mark the changes

One thing that's lacking at the moment is a crash cymbal to punctuate the end of every drum roll and the start of the section immediately following it. Load a crash cymbal into a ReDrum (you could use the one that's also holding the snare sample from earlier) and play a hit on the first beat of the main part of the track, as the piano comes in. This trick can be used throughout the track to add a little extra build-up. From here on, the arrangement can be a case of bringing things in and out, and adding automated filter sweeps strategically to form short breaks in the track. A little later on, you may want to swap the piano lead line for something else. There's a good Malstrom patch called 'Ebm lead', so load it up (Figure 9.9).

Copy and paste some of the material you already have so that there's a section with everything except the piano and drums. Leave it to play for eight bars or so, then add a leadline using the new Malstrom. This patch is perfect for trance and you should try playing some four note fast arpeggios that follow the chord sequence of the track. You can use a Matrix for this, but it's more fun to play it by hand. See the example for an idea of what works well. Also, add a little reverb and delay to the Malstrom, although not too much as the track is pretty busy already.

File stage 6

Figure 9.9
Alternative trance lead sounds

Figure 9.10
Running a Malstrom through insert effects

Figure 9.11
Arpeggiated notes — perfect for trance
leads

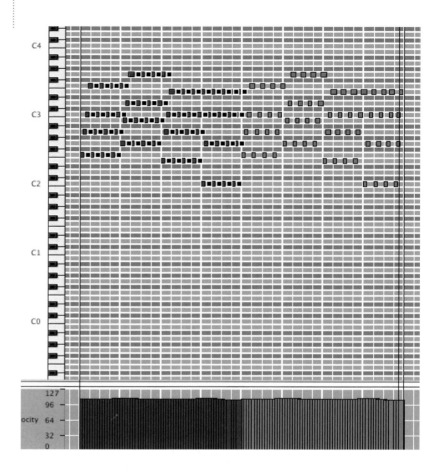

It's probably a good idea to do an automated filter sweep on the new lead line as it comes in, as you've been doing with other elements in this track. This time, just for variation, rather than using the filters on the synth itself, attach an ECF-42 filter to the Malstrom as an insert and automate its frequency knob, starting at zero and going up to 127. As it's an effect module, before you can automate any of its controls you'll need to right click or control-click on it and choose Create > Sequencer Track for Filter 1. This gives Reason somewhere in the sequencer to store the automation data for any non-instrument devices like effects, the Matrix or the mixer. As always you can do this by hand, or for more accuracy, using the pen or line tools in Edit view. Remember that if you paste these groups, the automation will be copied too, so quickly draw a value of 127 for the rest of the Filter's track, except if you want it to automate at other points.

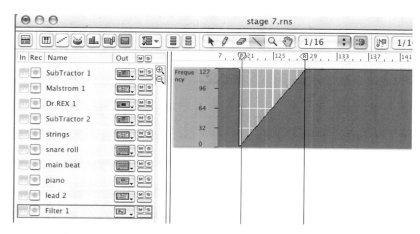

Figure 9.12
Automating filter sweeps

8 In the mix

If you're happy with your arrangement, it's time to mix. As usual this is very subjective, and will depend both on your preferences and the equipment you're listening on. Try adding a Mastering Combi between the Mixer and the Hardware Interface. Since the sound is already being quite heavily pumped, you don't always need to go mad with this. Try leaving the Default Mastering setting on, and just tweaking the MClass modules. You might have to make sure they're all switched on – some may be bypassed by default. Bear in mind that the way you mix on the desk will also affect the Mastering Combi, and vice versa. You can use the EQ on the mixer to iron out any inconsistencies in sounds, and to make them stand up or sit down in the mix. If the drums are being too heavily compressed and you're losing some of the bottom end, try lessening the compression a little and also boosting the lo and hi EQ on the desk just enough so the drums stand out, without appearing to sit on top of the rest of the track. Most of the synths will benefit from having their top end come through clearly. Trance synths (and trance music) can stand a lot more treble than most other styles – it's a hallmark of the genre. Needless to say though, they should still be well blended in the mix.

File stage 7

Figure 9.13
Getting the mix right

9 Master your style

The MClass Stereo Imager adds a great deal to the track without your even really having to tweak it all that much. The MClass Equalizer is a great way of fine tuning the whole mix after you've got all the levels set on the mixer. Invariably, a little sweetening is needed right at the end, a tiny amount of balancing of the lows, mids and high frequencies. Again, this is entirely dependent on your own tastes. If you're wondering what the Mastering Combi is adding, try bypassing it for a moment with its master bypass switch. You'll

be amazed – all the life will drop out of the sound. Make sure you switch it back on before you do your final mixdown!

Figure 9.14
Tweaking the Mastering Combi

Electropop

A brief history of electropop

Electropop is in many ways a variation of the sort of synth-based pop music that flourished in the late 1970s and into the 80s. Unlike a lot of that type of pop, it isn't dismissed as quickly for being inextricably linked with the 80s, and therefore very out-of-date. It also differs from synth-pop in having a harder, more electronic sound characterised by drum machines and (what are now) vintage synths.

Although a lot of the early pioneers of electropop used synths and sometimes even just consisted of a singer and a programmer, by blending these elements with a song-based structure rather than just music tracks they achieved considerable commercial success. Early adopters include Gary Numan, Kraftwerk, Erasure, the Pet Shop Boys, Soft Cell and even New Order in their poppier moments. Electropop went fairly quiet in the 1990s, a decade when indie and dance, and later nu-metal and R'n'B would dominate the charts. Some bands did persist though, notably Depeche Mode, the Pet Shop Boys and Eurythmics, all of whom are still going strong today.

Electropop has enjoyed something of a renaissance since the turn of the millennium, with bands like Fischerspooner, Ladytron and Freezepop updating the electropop sound and bringing it back to prominence. This is reflective of a wider use of vintage synthesizers and drum machines in mainstream music after their virtual disappearance outside the dance scene in the 90s. Nobody has done more to revitalise electropop than Goldfrapp, their second album *Black Cherry* and especially their third, *Supernature*, bringing lush production values back to the genre and at the same time finding a huge audience. Madonna's album *Confessions on a Dance Floor* has also taken on a lot of electropop elements and turned them into great commercial success.

Recommended listening
Fischerspooner - #1 (2002)
Goldfrapp – *Supernature* (2005)
Pet Shop Boys – *Actually* (1987)
Depeche Mode – *Some Great Reward* (1984)
Ladytron – *604* (2001)
Erasure – *Wild* (1989)

The Workshop

1 Getting started

Electropop tends to be fairly upbeat, so a tempo of around 130 is a good starting point. Remember that more often than not, drum machines will drive an electropop track and they don't sound that great when playing at a slow tempo, unless it's really slowly for a ballad. You could start by coming up with a riff to play on a synth, somewhere in the mid range. This music is often heavily riff-driven, so make sure it's something that is catchy that you will be able to develop later on. Try loading a Malstrom and looking for a sound – there's one in the Sound Bank called Breckerlead that sounds good. Quantize the notes fairly tightly – a setting of 1/16 and 100% should do it. See the example for an idea for a riff. You might also want to attach a Scream 4 to the Malstrom and warm up the sound a bit using something like the Tape preset. Try also adding a small amount of reverb and a Unison to fatten the synth up a little.

Figure 10.1
Fattening up synth sounds with a Unison

2 Building beats

Copy and paste a few groups of this riff so that you'll have something to build on. Add a ReDrum. After eight bars or so, bring in a lightweight beat. Look in the Electronic Kits folder on the Sound Bank and you'll find some good, old-school drum machines. They're all good – in the example, kit 2 is used.

File stage 1

Some of the most interesting beats come from experimenting with the step sequencer . More detailed instructions on how this works can be found in the chapter on House music. Try programming a beat into the ReDrum using the pads, a combination of different sounds. Copy and paste the successive beats into different sequencer slots on the ReDrum, building the beat up slightly with each new version. Then with each pattern selected, place the L and R locators over different sections of the track and select Edit > Copy Pattern To Track. Remember to then uncheck Enable Pattern Section on the ReDrum. All your patterns should now be in the main sequencer, and hopefully they build up, as in the example. To beef up the drums a little, attach a compressor, a Unison and a Scream 4 as inserts. Don't go mad with the distortion – use something subtle like the Tape preset. Also keep the size of the reverb and the amount applied fairly low. Use the Damp control on the RV-7 to control it.

Figure 10.2
Beefing up the drums

3 Adding harmonies

As the beat starts to build up you can begin to add another riff using another synth. Try a Combi this time. There's a good one on the Sound Bank called Ultrapulse, so load it up.

Play something that harmonises well with the first riff, in a similar key range. The Combi is already running through a fair few effects so you probably won't need to add any more. Let this go on for a while and then create a little variation before the main part of the track kicks in. This could be as simple as changing the notes slightly, varying them slightly from the originals. Copy in the drums too, but leave out the last bar to provide a brief gap

File stage 2

One Finger Triad.cmb
Pipeline.cmb
Poly-800 [with Mono VCF].cmb
Polywerk.cmb
Resotables.cmb
SawWorld.cmb
Toto meets DL Roth.cmb
UltraPulse.cmb
UltraSaw.cmb

Figure 10.3

Figure 10.4
Drop out the beats before a change in the track

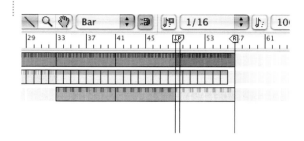

before the main drums will come in. A good trick here with the melody is to have both synth lines end on the same note, as in the example.

4 Electronic kits

File stage 3

Now skip past the part you were just working on and create a main beat for the body of the track. Create another ReDrum and load up a bigger kit. The one called Nanoloop Kit 1 sounds great for this kind of music.

Figure 10.5
Choosing electronic kits

Name	Modified	
Electronic Kit 1.drp	2 Feb 2005 15:56	
Electronic Kit 2.drp	2 Feb 2005 15:56	
Electronic Kit 3.drp	2 Feb 2005 15:56	
Electronic Kit 4.drp	2 Feb 2005 15:56	
Electronic Kit 5.drp	2 Feb 2005 15:56	
Electronic Kit 6.drp	2 Feb 2005 15:56	
Grain Kit.drp	2 Feb 2005 15:56	
Hard&Soft Kit.drp	2 Feb 2005 15:56	
Ingredients Kit.drp	2 Feb 2005 15:56	
Lantern Kit.drp	2 Feb 2005 15:56	
Nanoloop Kit 1.drp	2 Feb 2005 15:56	
Nanoloop Kit 2.drp	2 Feb 2005 15:56	
Obex Kit.drp	2 Feb 2005 15:56	

It also has some great bleep samples as part of the kit, which fit really well into a beat in this kind of music. You can of course record a beat simply by looping a section and playing the ReDrum by hand, quantizing afterwards to iron out any timing problems. This bypasses the step sequencer altogether. For added punch, why not try adding an effect Combi to the new ReDrum. Try the preset called Body&Punchy Snare from the Dynamics > Drums folder.

Figure 10.6
Adding an effect Combi to a drum kit for extra punch

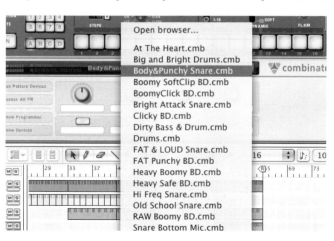

The preset is great but if anything, a bit too loud. Try opening the Combi up by pressing its Show Devices button. You can improve the sound by dropping the Compressor's ratio a little, and also by activating the Maximizer and switching on its Soft Clip button.

Figure 10.7
Tweaking the Combi

You should probably also add a small amount of reverb to the main beat. Again, keep it tight, not too roomy.

5 Big basses

At this point the track is crying out for a bassline to come in with the main drum beat to give the transition some added kick. Create a Subtractor and try out the patch called BassQue from the Sound Bank. It works well, so play in a bassline. Something simple will do, maybe just alternating octaves with a bit of variation thrown in. It's worth attaching a Compressor to the Subtractor to make sure the bottom end of the synth doesn't get too murky. One thing the track is still lacking is something to carry it along a bit more – it still sounds slightly choppy. You could do this with more hi hats, or with a tambourine. Load up a Dr.REX player and locate a tambourine REX loop from the Sound Bank. There's one called Tamb_05b_120 that works well. Use the

File stage 4

Figure 10.8
A tambourine REX loop – quick and easy

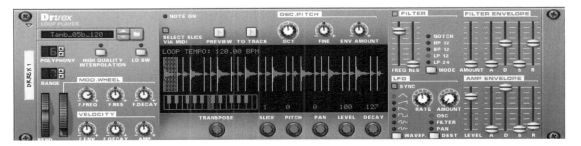

To Track button on the Dr.REX to get the data onto the sequencer track. Use the Filter Freq control on the Dr.REX to roll off a little of the top end so it sits better in the mix. Remember this is supposed to be fairly lo-fi stuff.

6 Break it down

File stage 5

Copy and paste some of this main part of the track so it extends over as many bars as you feel appropriate. Then, to add some interest, copy and paste the break you created earlier and alter the bassline to fit with it. You may have to play a new section of bass to follow the different pattern in the break. Let this play for eight bars or so, then try a breakdown. Create a Subtractor and find some empty space in the sequencer. Load up a patch called Fonky dude from the Sound Bank. In the empty space, play in a variation on the themes from earlier in the track. It doesn't matter if it sounds a bit artificial at the moment – it won't when the drums come in.

Figure 10.9
Alternative lead lines

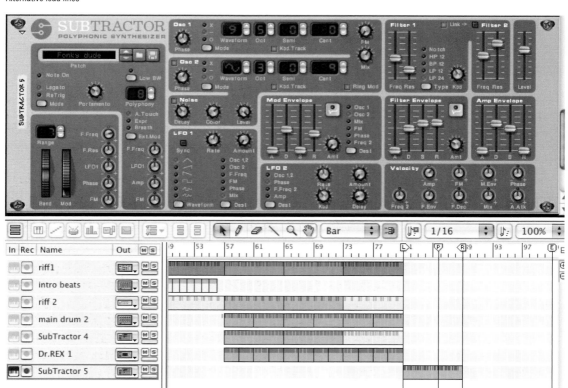

At this point you could program another beat for the break like before, or you could try a REX loop. Create a Dr.REX and browse through the ReFills folder to see what you can find. Inside Zero G ReFills > Planet of the Breaks > REX Loops there's one called 'HitTheBreak4 4bar' that sounds great. Load it and send it to the track as before over the break. It will occupy eight bars and two groups. To add some instant variation, you could try selecting the second group of notes and choosing Edit > Change events. Clicking the Alter Notes > Apply button will create a different pattern while retaining the tim-

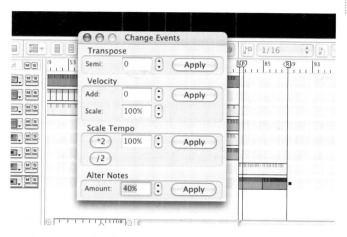

Figure 10.10
Use Change Events to add variations

ing. This is a good way to make Reason add pattern variations to anything, from drums to basses. You could try altering some of the groups of the main beat using the same method.

After the break, try bringing the main part of the track back in by pasting it.

7 Pad it out

As the track develops, you could try adding a pad sound to sit behind the rest of the instruments and just fill it out a bit. A Malstrom patch will do it – there's one called 'Heaven' that is just lo-fi and subtle enough to work here. Try using it to just shadow the chord changes, very simply. A single, held chord on each chord change will do it.

Try also adding another synth line to complement the others that are playing. There are some great Malstrom patches in the Sound Bank – one called 'JunoLead' works well, especially when run through a Unison. Playing something simple will make sure you don't overcomplicate the track. Try also attaching a DDl-1 delay and applying a tiny amount of delay. A dry / wet setting of around 7 is a good one to choose. Use the EQ on the mixer channel for the Malstrom to roll off a little of the bottom end, as this will make the sound sit better in the mix.

8 Start to mix

As electropop is song-based, you might well want to ReWire Reason together with another sequencer like Logic, Cubase or Sonar in order to record some live vocals. If you are going to do this, the arrangement of the track will depend heavily on how the vocals are going to fit with it. Assuming that you have got an arrangement that you are happy with, move on to mixing the track.

Add a Mastering Combi between the mixer and the Hardware Interface. Try loading up the Pop preset. It's good but lacks some bottom end for an electropop production. Open up the Combi by pressing its Show Devices button. Loop up a section of the track and use the EQ module to raise the gain of the bottom end a bit.

File stage 6

Figure 10.11
Simple pad chords

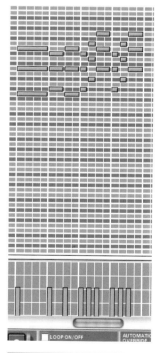

File stage 7

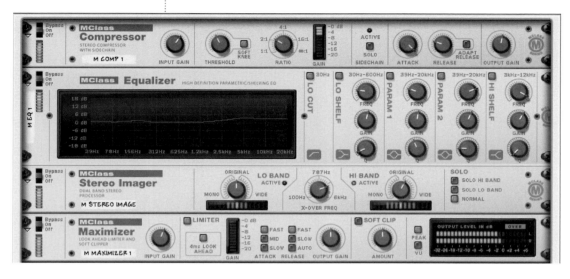

Figure 10.12
Tweaking the Mastering Combi

Figure 10.13
Use the controls on the ReDrum to
balance the kit

You may also want to boost the lower and upper mids slightly to squeeze a bit more range out of the sound. The top end can stand pushing a little too, if you think it needs it. Using the mixer's faders and EQ, make sure the bass drum is punchy enough. If necessary, go back to the ReDrum and use the individual level controls on each of its channels to balance out the kit. Remember that you have the option of routing each ReDrum channel out separately to the desk, and via additional effects if you want. You can also boost EQs slightly and drop faders slightly to keep sounds prominent without them being too loud. Ensure that the hi-hats don't take over the track, as they can sometimes do, by backing them off slightly on the ReDrum itself.

File stage 8

If any elements seem to jump out of the track too much, put a compressor on them and see if that helps. For example, if the Malstrom at the start of the track is quite loud when playing by itself, try the compressor trick. You might have to do this with the Subtractor that plays in the breaks as well. Finally, try adding an MClass Stereo Imager between the Mastering Combi and the Hardware Interface. You should find that this gives the track an even better sense of sheen and stereo width.

Exporting from Reason

So you've spent ages on building and automating your tracks, and now it's time to export them so you can put them on CD and play them to the world. There are two ways in which you can do this – by recording the track to a realtime media like a CD recorder, DAT or MiniDisc, or by exporting it to an audio file. The latter is by far the most common with Reason, but here's a quick description of how you might do it using the first method.

Exporting in realtime

This used to be the accepted way of mixing down before computers became so commonplace. Basically it just means playing the track out in realtime and recording it to some kind of magnetic or optical media like a tape or CD. It is a perfectly acceptable way of mixing down, although in reality, now that every computer has a CD burner, and you're more likely to want to upload mp3s of your work, it often makes sense to export straight to computer's hard drive. One case in which you would almost certainly need to record out to DAT or CD in realtime is if you have routed Reason's tracks out directly through your audio interface by manually patching channels through the Hardware Interface. In this situation you may well be processing Reason's

Figure 11.1
If you are routing audio from Reason out through your soundcard's separate outputs, realtime mixdown may well be the way to go

tracks through external hardware effects and a mixer, and those effects would only be recorded if the total summed output of Reason (main stereo outs plus any separated channels) were all collected together and recorded on a single device.

Mixdown is a good time to apply a fade in or fade out to your track. This is done by automating the master fader. As you record, move the fader smoothly up or down. Alternatively, open

Figure 11.2
Automate the master fader for a smooth
fade out

the automation subtrack for the master fader by alt or control-clicking on it.
Then draw automation in with the Pen tool or, better still, with the Line tool
to create a smooth ramp. Remember that to automate anything on the mixer
you must first create a sequencer track for it.

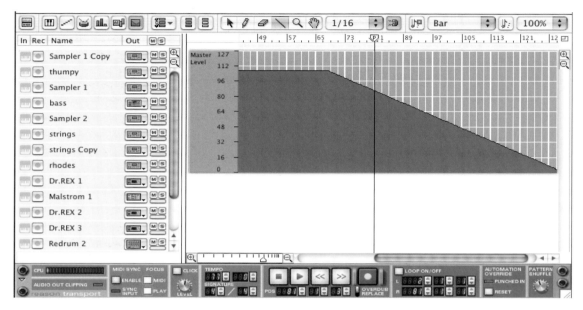

A Note About ReWire

If you are running Reason in ReWire mode with Sonar, Cubase, Logic or any
other compatible program, Reason's audio outs are inextricably linked with
that program. The export options in Reason will be greyed out as they can't
operate independently of the host program. In this case, selecting audio mixdown in the host program will include Reason's output in its mixdown, meaning you don't have to worry about it.

Figure 11.3
In ReWire mode, Reason's export options
are transferred to the host program,
such as Cubase

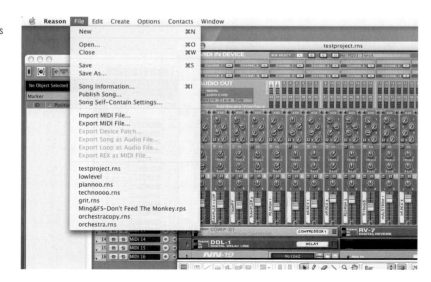

Checking everything

After you have perfected the levels and the automation for your track, make sure the left and right markers are positioned over the start and finish of your track. Leave at least one bar of empty space either side. If your track ends with an echoing sound of any kind, make sure to leave a few bars of space, or it will be cut off. If you need more space on the timeline, drag the E marker further to the right (Figure 11.4).

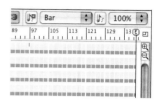

Figure 11.4
If you need more space, drag the End marker to the right

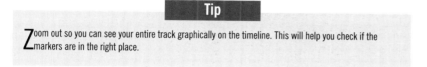

Tip

Zoom out so you can see your entire track graphically on the timeline. This will help you check if the markers are in the right place.

Make sure everything that should be unmuted is unmuted. Select File > Export Song as Audio File. Choose somewhere sensible to put it. If you're on a Mac, choose the AIFF format. On a PC, choose WAVE. For audio CD you'll want to select a sample rate of 44.1kHz and a bit depth of 16 bit.

Figure 11.5
Choose an audio output format depending on your platform of choice

As a rule of thumb, don't go above or below these settings unless you know why you need to. Most video editing programs run at 48KHz but can happily deal with audio sampled at 44.1. If you are exporting to 16 bits you can tick the Dither box, which will make sure there's no distortion introduced by changing bit depths. Reason now renders down your track, including all the effects and automation, to a single file. If the track is long and has lots of effects and instruments, this might take a moment or two.

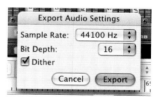

Figure 11.6
The Dither option in Reason 3, to ensure clean bit rate conversion

If for some reason you need every track as an individual file, for remixing purposes, you can simply solo up one track at a time and export it. This is a bit time-intensive, and is better achieved by using ReWire to record tracks simultaneously through into a host sequencer, if you have the software.

If you haven't already inserted one, it's a good idea to put an MClass mastering Combi between the mixer and the Hardware Interface and select or modify a preset that suits your music best. The changes to the sound introduced by the MClass effects are included in the mixdown. You'll be surprised by how much bigger and wider it can make your track sound.

Figure 11.7
Introduce a mastering Combi between the Mixer and the Hardware Interface to improve the overall sound of a mix

Figure 11.8

There are some other export options worth mentioning.

- Export MIDI file will export the entire track as a MIDI file, ideal for sharing over the internet or for backing up.

- Export Device Patch will export the current patch of whichever device you have selected. This is really just another way of performing the save function from the front of the modules.
- Export REX as MIDI file will create a file containing just the MIDI data contained in a REX loop, not the audio.
- Export Loop as audio file is especially useful if you are taking small sections of music into other programs to work with. For instance, if you have a great drum loop, you probably only need four bars of it to take into Pro Tools to do a remix. Or, for multimedia purposes where small loops are necessary for quick download speeds, taking a bit of something is easier than taking it all. Remember when you do any kind of export

from Reason that what gets exported is what's audible. That is, if you don't want certain tracks to be present in the exported audio file, you have to mute them. Anything that's muted will be left out.

If you are working on different machines, remember that you must have the same sets of sounds present on all machines for projects to play back properly. You can use the Search and Proceed warning box that pops up to find the files, but only if they're on the system somewhere. If you are using lots of your own samples and moving around it's a good idea to use the ReFill Packer that comes with Reason to organize them into ReFills, which are easy to manage.

Sharing and publishing

If you choose to upload your songs to the web or send them to anyone, there are steps you can take to ensure your work is identified as your own. Here are some tips for publishing songs.

If you choose File > Song Self-Contain Settings, you can see exactly what parts of what ReFills you are using in your track. This window displays audio files, not patches. Remember that Reason project files are just instructions – they don't include any audio data. For this reason, you have to make sure that if you are sending someone the file as a Reason project rather than an mp3, you must also include any relevant ReFills. Otherwise, when they open it they will just be prompted to locate the missing files. Projects will still open, but any missing files will be replaced by silence.

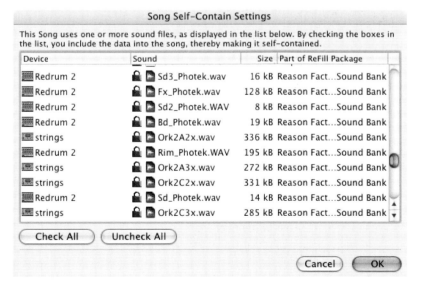

Figure 11.9

By selecting File > Song Information you can embed data about yourself and your music. You can select a 256x256 pixel image, enter your URL and email and some text of you like. If you choose to show the Splash window on open, it will always pop up when the song is loaded.

Figure 11.10
Embed text, URL and email information and your choice of picture in your song file

Regular Reason project files can be modified by whoever opens them. However, if you don't want anyone to be able to mess with your work, choose File > Publish Song. What you then create is an .rps file which can be opened and edited but not saved. Also, if the song is edited in any way, it cannot be exported as audio until it has been quit and re-opened in its original form. This means that it's impossible (or at least very hard) for anyone to remix your track or change it without your permission. Interestingly, the option to export patches is also greyed out in .rps files, meaning that if you have created a killer synth sound, nobody can steal it – unless you want them to!

Figure 11.11
A published Reason song is relatively well protected against changes or borrowing of patches

On the whole there are no cross-platform issues between Reason on a PC or Mac. A Reason file is just a Reason file, and that's that. As there are no plugins to deal with, that's not a problem either. The only possible incompatibility is if you have some audio files on one system but not another. Be aware also that you can't open files made in a newer version of Reason in an older version of the software. If you are working in Version 3, stick with it. If you're working in version 2.5, don't start working in version 3 unless you are prepared to switch permanently.

Index